A QUICK REVIEW OF U.S. HISTORY AND GOVERNMENT

Third Edition

Everything You Need to Know to Pass the Regents Examination

JAMES KILLORAN
STUART ZIMMER
MARK JARRETT, Ph.D.

JARRETT PUBLISHING COMPANY

East Coast Office:
P.O. Box 1460
Ronkonkoma, NY 11779
631-981-4248

Florida Office:
50 Nettles Blvd.
Jensen Beach, FL 34957
1-800-859-7679

West Coast Office:
10 Folin Lane
Lafayette, CA 94549
925-906-9742

1-800-859-7679 • Fax 631-588-4722 • www.jarrettpub.com

Jarrett Publishing Company
P.O. Box 1460
Ronkonkoma, New York 11779

ISBN 1-882422-56-2

Copyright 2015 Jarrett Publishing Company
Printed in the United States of America by
Malloy, Inc., Ann Arbor, Michigan

Third Edition
10 9 8 7 6 5 4 3 2   16 15

ACKNOWLEDGEMENTS

Layout and typesetting by Maple Hill Press, Huntington, NY.

This book is dedicated

...to my wife Donna, my children Christian, Carrie and Jesse, and
my grandson Aiden — *James Killoran*

...to my wife Joan, my children Todd and Ronald,
and my grandchildren Jared and Katie — *Stuart Zimmer*

...to my wife Goska and my children Alexander and Julia — *Mark Jarrett*

ABOUT THE AUTHORS

James Killoran, a retired Assistant Principal, has written many social studies books. He has extensive experience in test writing for the N.Y. State Board of Regents in social studies and has served on the Committee for Testing of the National Council of Social Studies. His article on social studies testing has been published in *Social Education*, the country's leading social studies journal. Mr. Killoran has won many awards for outstanding teaching and curriculum development, including "Outstanding Social Studies Teacher" and "Outstanding Social Studies Supervisor" in New York City. In 1993, he was awarded an Advanced Certificate for Teachers of Social Studies by the N.C.S.S. In 1997, he served as Chairman of the N.C.S.S. Committee on Awarding Advanced Certificates for Teachers of Social Studies.

Stuart Zimmer, a retired social studies teacher, has written numerous social studies books. He served as a test writer for the N.Y. State Board of Regents in Social Studies, and has written for the National Merit Scholarship Examination. He has published numerous articles on teaching and testing in social studies journals. He has presented many demonstrations and educational workshops at state and national teachers' conferences. In 1989, Mr. Zimmer's achievements were recognized by the New York State Legislature with a Special Legislative Resolution in his honor.

Mark Jarrett, a former social studies teacher, has written many social studies books. Mr. Jarrett has served as a test writer for the N.Y. State Board of Regents, and has taught at Hofstra University. He was educated at Columbia University, the London School of Economics, the Law School of the University of California at Berkeley, and Stanford University. Mr. Jarrett has received several academic awards including the Order of the Coif at Berkeley and the David and Christina Phelps Harris Fellowship at Stanford. He worked as an attorney for ten years with the international law firm of Baker & McKenzie.

TABLE OF CONTENTS

CHAPTER 1

THE BASIC TOOLS OF AMERICAN HISTORY

SKIPPING THE FIRST THREE CHAPTERS COULD BE HAZARDOUS TO YOUR SUCCESS!

OVERVIEW

This book is designed to provide a quick review for the **U.S. History and Government Regents Examination**. This introductory chapter provides techniques to help you remember important information. The next chapter will help you answer thematic essay questions. Chapter 3 focuses on how to answer document-based essay questions.

Later chapters of the book provide short content reviews summarizing the major developments in American history. Each content review chapter opens with a page identifying the main themes of the period. After a review of the content, the chapter closes with a series of sample test questions. Following the content review chapters is a final review that includes:

- a checklist of the most notable Americans tested on the Regents
- the most important terms and concepts of U.S. history and government
- charts listing major milestones in U.S. history

The book concludes with a full-length practice U.S. History and Government examination, similar to an actual Regents Examination.

REMEMBERING INFORMATION

Examination questions often test your knowledge of important terms, concepts and people in American history and government. This section discusses ways to make it easier for you to remember important information so that you can improve your performance on the U.S. History and Government Regents Examination.

TERMS

Terms refer to specific things that actually happened or existed, such as particular places or events. Questions about a term usually ask about its main features:

what it is (or was)   *its purpose*   *its causes and effects*   *its significance*

CONCEPTS

Concepts are words or phrases that refer to categories of information. They allow us to organize large amounts of information. For example, the American Revolution, the War of 1812 and the Civil War share common characteristics. The concept *war* acts as an umbrella, grouping these specific "examples" by identifying what they have in common. Questions about concepts usually ask for a definition or an example of the concept. When you study a concept, you should learn the following:

its definition   *an example*

FAMOUS PEOPLE

In American history you will also learn about many famous people. Test questions about these individuals will usually ask you who they are and why they are famous. Therefore, when you study a famous person, it is important to learn:

the place and time period in which the person lived   *his or her background or position*   *the person's accomplishment or impact*

To help you remember important terms, concepts and people, you should complete an index card for each one. Here is the information each card should contain:

❖ **Front of Card**: Write out the important information *(see page 2)*.

❖ **Back (or front) of Card**: Draw a picture about the information. Turning written information into an illustration helps you to clarify its meaning. The ability to change a term or concept from one medium *(words)* into another *(an illustration)* is only possible if you *truly* understand the term or concept.

Look at the following completed index card for a term:

DECLARATION OF INDEPENDENCE

WHAT IS IT? A document written mainly by Thomas Jefferson in 1776.

PURPOSE: It declared America's independence from Britain.

SIGNIFICANCE: It established the basic principle upon which the U.S. government is based — that government is created by a group of citizens to protect their rights.

(Your drawing may appear on the front or on the back of the card.)

ANSWERING DATA-BASED QUESTIONS

Knowing how to interpret different types of data is crucial to performing well on multiple-choice and document-based essay questions. Some questions will present their own data in the question. The types of data most often found on these questions are:

• Maps   • Line Graphs   • Tables   • Political Cartoons   • Speaker Questions
• Bar Graphs • Pie Charts   • Timelines   • Outlines   • Reading Passages

Almost all data-based questions can be grouped into four general types — (1) comprehension; (2) conclusion; (3) explanation; and (4) prediction.

COMPREHENSION QUESTIONS

These questions ask you to find a specific item, figure, or number presented in the data. A comprehension question may take various forms, such as:

❖ According to the chart, in which year was cotton production the greatest?

❖ In 1830, the greatest population growth occurred in which area of the country?

CONCLUSION OR GENERALIZATION QUESTIONS

These questions ask you to draw a *conclusion* or make a *generalization* by tying together several elements found in the data presented. These questions may take various forms, such as:

❖ Which generalization is most accurate, based on the data?

❖ What is the main idea of the data?

EXPLANATION QUESTIONS

These questions ask you to provide an *explanation* for the situation illustrated by the data. Such questions may take various forms, such as:

❖ The problem illustrated in the cartoon was caused by ...

❖ Which factor contributed most to the change shown on the graph?

PREDICTION QUESTIONS

These questions ask you to make a *prediction* based on the situation illustrated in the data. Such questions may take various forms, such as:

❖ Which may be an effect of the situation shown in the data?

❖ Based on the information in the data, which is most likely to occur?

DEVELOPING A SENSE OF TIME AND PLACE

It is very important to have a good grasp of **time** and **place** when studying U.S. history and government.

- You must have a strong general sense of the basic time periods of American history, including the major beliefs, ideas, technologies, and events of each period, in order to understand particular events and facts in their proper context.

- You must know the main geographical features of the United States, since they provide the "stage" on which developments in U.S. history unfolded.

DEVELOPING A SENSE OF TIME

Historians often divide history into **time periods** — spans of time unified by common characteristics. There is no exact agreement on historical periods and their dates. Traditionally, historical periods have been tied to a particular event or movement. This book emphasizes events that have occurred since the Civil War, just as the Regents Examination does. The book therefore divides the history of the United States into eight time periods, each with its own unique features:

> 1. Constitutional Foundations, from the 1500s to 1787
> 2. The Constitution Tested, from 1787 to 1877
> 3. The Rise of Industry, from 1877 to 1898
> 4. The Progressive Era, from 1898 to 1920
> 5. Prosperity and Depression, from 1920 to 1941
> 6. The Age of Global Crisis, from 1941 to 1950
> 7. The World in Uncertain Times, from 1950 to 1972
> 8. Contemporary America, from 1972 to the present

Based on your previous study of American history, you should be able to identify some of the major characteristics of each of these time periods.

DEVELOPING A SENSE OF PLACE

The United States is located in the middle of the continent of North America, and extends from the Atlantic to the Pacific Ocean. In addition to the continental United States, the United States includes Alaska and Hawaii. Cut off from much of the world by two large oceans, America's location separated Native American Indians from the cultures of Africa and Eurasia. Later in history, the people of the United States felt protected from the problems of the rest of the world by these two vast oceans.

— REGIONS OF THE CONTINENTAL UNITED STATES —

A **region** is an area that shares certain features and that has greater contact with other places within the region than with the outside. Because of its diverse topography (*surface features*) and climate, the continental United States can be thought of as one nation consisting of several geographic regions:

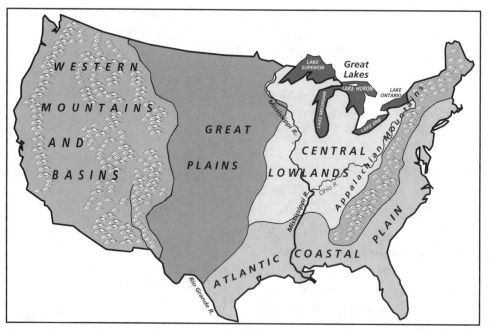

THE ATLANTIC COASTAL PLAIN
The **Atlantic Coastal Plain** is one of the world's largest coastal plains. It stretches southward from New England to Georgia, and then turns southwest, widening out to Texas. This was the region first settled by colonists from Europe in the 1700s. Much of the area was forest before settlers turned it into farmland. Today, it is the region

with the highest concentration of Americans. The Atlantic Coastal Plain rises up to a hilly area, known as the Piedmont, as it approaches the Appalachian Mountains.

THE APPALACHIAN MOUNTAINS

The **Appalachian Mountains** cover much of the eastern part of the United States. They extend from Maine in the north to Alabama in the south, where they are cut off by the coastal plain. In the south, the Allegheny Mountains, the Blue Ridge Mountains and the Great Smoky Mountains are part of the Appalachians. The Appalachians were difficult for the first settlers to pass through because they presented an almost unbroken mountain chain with few gaps.

THE CENTRAL LOWLANDS

To the west of the Appalachians are the **Central Lowlands**. The northern part of this region was once scraped by glaciers *(huge moving sheets of ice)* and is a continuation of a sheet of ancient rocks extending down from Canada. The Superior Uplands in Minnesota and Northern Michigan and the Adirondack Mountains in Northern New York are part of the system. Farther south, where the elevation is lower, glaciers and winds deposited rich soil, making the land well suited for farming. Parts of the Central Lowlands are among the most fertile regions in the nation. The eastern part of the Central Lowlands are grasslands and wildflowers, known as prairies.

THE GREAT PLAINS

West of the Mississippi, the grasslands become much drier and more hilly. This region is known as the **Great Plains**. These plains were once covered with sod and thick grasses. The Central Lowlands and the Great Plains are the world's most productive farm and grazing land, providing vast amounts of corn, wheat, and livestock.

THE WESTERN MOUNTAINS AND BASINS

West of the Great Plains the land rises sharply, forming the Rocky Mountains. These mountains extend from western Canada as far south as New Mexico. Still further west are the Cascade and Sierra Nevada Ranges, and the Pacific Coastal Ranges. These western areas receive little rainfall. The Great Basin, separating the Rocky Mountains and the Sierra Nevada, is dry and desert-like. California's Central Valley, located between the Sierra Nevada and the Coastal Range, has excellent soils, almost continuous sunshine, and a long growing season. Although the Central Valley gets little rainfall in summer, irrigation has been made it into very productive farmland.

CHAPTER 2

HOW TO ANSWER
THEMATIC ESSAY QUESTIONS

An essay question measures your ability to present information in written form. The **U.S. History and Government Regents** will include one thematic essay.

THEMATIC ESSAY QUESTIONS

A thematic essay requires you to focus on a particular theme or generalization. Let's look at a typical thematic essay question:

Directions: Write a well-organized essay that includes an introduction, several paragraphs addressing the task below, and a conclusion.

Theme: Diversity

> The struggles of various groups in this nation to gain civil rights has been a constant theme of U. S. history

Task:

Choose *one* group from your study of U.S. history and government

For the *one* group selected:
- *Describe* how that group was once denied its civil rights.
- *Discuss* one or more actions taken by an individual, a group or the government to overcome this denial of civil rights.
- *Discuss* the impact of these actions.

You may use any example from your study of U.S. history and government. Some suggestions you might wish to consider include: Native American Indians, women, African Americans, Japanese Americans, Hispanic Americans, and persons with disabilities.
You are *not* limited to these suggestions.

Notice how a thematic essay question opens with the *Directions*. They tell you the form in which the essay must be written. Next is a *Theme* — stated as a **generalization** — that identifies a common pattern. In this example, the generalization states that various groups in America have struggled to gain their civil rights. The question then gives you a *Task* to complete. The Task contains specific informational requirements. The *suggestions* provide examples of groups that you might choose to write about.

Thus, in each thematic essay question, you will be asked:

★ to show your understanding of a generalization by using specific examples that support it, and

★ to write a well-organized essay that includes an introduction, several paragraphs that address the Task, and a conclusion.

THE "QUESTION WORDS" OF ESSAY QUESTIONS

In essay questions, the exact instructions for what you are supposed to do in writing your answer are contained in the *question words*. The most common are:

Describe or Discuss   *Explain or Show How*   *Explain or Show Why*

In this section, we will explore the meaning of each of these "question words."

DESCRIBE/DISCUSS

Describe or **discuss** means to "tell about something." Describe or discuss is used when you must write about the **"who," "what," "when,"** and **"where"** of something. Not every "describe" or "discuss" question will require all four of these elements. Let's look at two examples:

★ *Describe* an achievement of the Progressive Era.
★ *Discuss* two changes brought about by the Civil War.

Note how the first question asks you to *describe* an achievement of the Progressive Era. Your answer should include **who** (*Progressives*), **what** (*introduced many reforms, such as direct primaries*), **when** (*early 1900s*), and **where** (*in many states, and nationally*). **Hint**: When asked to *describe* or *discuss* something, go through a mental checklist of *who*, *what*, *when*, and *where*.

EXPLAIN AND SHOW

Explain and *show* are often linked with the additional word *how* or *why*. The key in approaching any question with these question words is to determine whether the question requires you to give an answer for *how* something happened or *why* it happened.

❖ **HOW QUESTIONS.** These questions ask you to explain how something works or how it relates to something else. Let's look at two examples:

★ *Show how* the New Deal had a lasting impact on the nation.
★ *Explain how* improvements in technology can affect a country's social and economic development.

Notice how the first question requires you to provide specific information and examples to *show how* the statement is true. The facts you mention might include the following: (1) Americans gave up their traditional belief that everybody can make it on their own, even in an economic depression; (2) the federal government intervened more directly in the economy with programs such as the Civilian Conservation Corps and Social Security; (3) public expectations of the Presidency changed. **Hint:** Be sure that these parts of your answer (*the information and examples*) "support" the general statement, and that the general statement answers the question.

❖ **WHY QUESTIONS.** *Explain why* and *show why* questions focus on causes — the reasons why. Your answer should identify the reasons why an event or relationship took place and briefly describe each reason. Two examples of such questions are:

★ *Explain why* the United States created the Marshall Plan.
★ *Show why* the Southern states seceded from the Union in 1860-1861.

Notice how the first question asks you to *explain* the reasons **why** the United States created the Marshall Plan. The following reasons *explain why*: (1) the fear among Americans that Communism would spread throughout Europe; (2) the need to build strong future trading partners for the United States; (3) the desire to help our European allies rebuild their economies after World War II. **Hint:** when asked to *explain why*, go through a mental checklist of various reasons or causes. Be sure the reasons and causes add up to a satisfactory explanation.

WRITING A WELL-ORGANIZED ESSAY

Let's practice writing a thematic essay by answering the model question on page 8.

❖ Start by looking at the **Task**. Be sure you understand what it asks you to do.
❖ Focus on what you need to do by <u>underlining</u> the "question words."
❖ Circle the *number of examples* the Task requires.

NOTES FOR YOUR ESSAY

Pre-writing notes help you organize your essay.

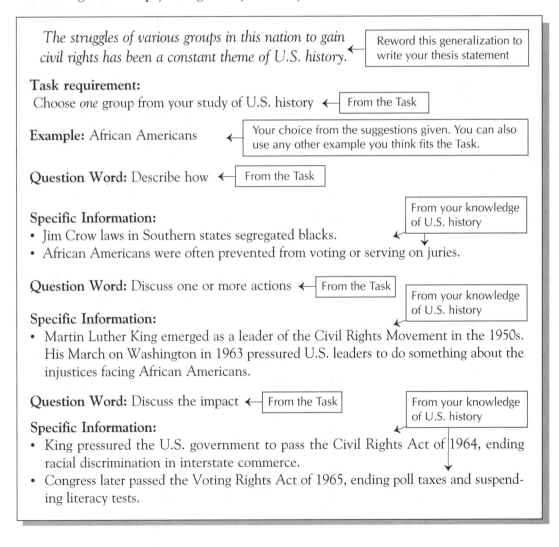

The struggles of various groups in this nation to gain civil rights has been a constant theme of U.S. history. ← Reword this generalization to write your thesis statement

Task requirement:
Choose *one* group from your study of U.S. history ← From the Task

Example: African Americans ← Your choice from the suggestions given. You can also use any other example you think fits the Task.

Question Word: Describe how ← From the Task

Specific Information: ← From your knowledge of U.S. history
• Jim Crow laws in Southern states segregated blacks.
• African Americans were often prevented from voting or serving on juries.

Question Word: Discuss one or more actions ← From the Task ← From your knowledge of U.S. history

Specific Information:
• Martin Luther King emerged as a leader of the Civil Rights Movement in the 1950s. His March on Washington in 1963 pressured U.S. leaders to do something about the injustices facing African Americans.

Question Word: Discuss the impact ← From the Task ← From your knowledge of U.S. history

Specific Information:
• King pressured the U.S. government to pass the Civil Rights Act of 1964, ending racial discrimination in interstate commerce.
• Congress later passed the Voting Rights Act of 1965, ending poll taxes and suspending literacy tests.

USING THE "CHEESEBURGER" METHOD

Now let's use the information from your notes to write a thematic essay. One way of organizing your response is to imagine your answer resembles a cheeseburger. The "top bun" is your **introduction**. The "cheese slice" forms a **transition sentence** into the main part of your essay. The "patties of meat" make up the **body of the essay** with your supporting information. The "bottom bun" is your **conclusion**.

TOP BUN *(INTRODUCTION)*

Your introduction should provide your **thesis statement** — the main theme of your essay. The thesis statement allows the reader of your essay to know exactly what you will be writing about and your viewpoint. If you have trouble creating your own thesis statement, you can use the generalization provided in the question and express it as an affirmative statement.

These two parts make up your first paragraph

CHEESE SLICE *(TRANSITION SENTENCE)*

The "cheese slice" sentence connects your introduction, with its thesis statement, to the specific information you provide in the main part of your essay. This sentence also leads the reader to the body of your essay, allowing the reader to follow your thoughts.

PATTIES OF MEAT *(BODY OF YOUR ESSAY)*

This section of the cheeseburger is the main part of your essay. Here, you give specific information — examples and facts — to support your thesis statement. Each group of facts and examples focusing on a specific bulleted part of the *Task* should be in its own paragraph. Notice how each of the three main paragraphs of the cheeseburger graphic on the next page correspond to the three requirements listed in the *Task*.

BOTTOM BUN *(CONCLUSION)*

The last part of your essay should reaffirm your thesis statement, except that it is now expressed as a conclusion. There are several ways to introduce your conclusion:

Therefore, we can see that ...   — **or** —   *Thus, it is clear that ...*

The conclusion may also include a brief summary of your key points. Notice how the closing sentence reminds the reader of your thesis statement and informs the reader that the essay has come to an end.

Now let's see how a model essay is organized along these lines:

Introduction, with thesis statement →

Our Declaration of Independence and Constitution promised equality to all Americans. Nevertheless, the struggle by some groups to gain their civil rights has been a constant theme of American history. African Americans were one group that struggled to gain their civil rights.

First paragraph

Transition sentence →

This essay will examine how African Americans were denied their civil rights, how Dr. Martin Luther King, Jr. and others led a movement to overcome this injustice, and how their actions led to the passage of new laws to protect civil rights.

This paragraph answers the first bulleted item →

African Americans were freed from slavery by the Civil War, but white Southerners denied them their civil rights after Reconstruction. "Jim Crow" laws in Southern states segregated blacks from whites in schools and most other public places. They also lost their right to vote because of poll taxes and literacy tests.

This paragraph covers the second bulleted item →

In the 1950s, Dr. King and other leaders launched the Civil Rights Movement. The NAACP gained an important victory in the *Brown v. Board of Education* case. The Supreme Court ruled that segregation in public schools was unconstitutional. Dr. King also helped lead the Montgomery bus boycott, protesting the arrest of Rosa Parks for refusing to give up her seat on a bus to a white person. This boycott ended racial segregation on the buses of Montgomery, Alabama. In 1963, Dr. King and others held a March on Washington, making Americans aware of the need for federal laws to prevent further injustices.

Three main paragraphs

This paragraph focuses on the impact →

As a result of these actions, Congress passed the Civil Rights Act of 1964 and the Voting Rights Act of 1965. Hotels, railroads, restaurants, and other businesses in interstate commerce could no longer discriminate against African Americans. Southern states could no longer make it difficult for their African American citizens to vote.

The success of the Civil Rights Movement thus had a deep impact on American society. As a result, new opportunities were opened for African Americans, while other groups like women followed the example set by Dr. King and others in seeking equal rights.

Conclusion

CHAPTER 3

HOW TO ANSWER DOCUMENT-BASED ESSAY QUESTIONS

The U.S. History and Government Regents will require you to answer one document-based essay, sometimes referred to as a "D.B.Q." This type of question tests your ability to interpret historical documents and data. Let's begin by looking at a simplified document-based essay question on the Industrial Revolution.

A SAMPLE QUESTION

This question is designed to test your ability to work with historical documents, and is based on the accompanying documents (1-4). Some of the documents have been edited for the purposes of the question. As you analyze the documents, take into account both the source of each document and any point of view that may be presented in the document.

Historical Context: Beginning in the 1890s, Americans set out to correct the problems caused by rapid industrial growth. Reformers worked to eliminate abuses and other problems caused by the rise of industry.

Task:
Using information from the documents and your knowledge of U.S. history, answer the questions that follow each document in Part A. Your answers to the questions will help you write the Part B essay, in which you will be asked to:

Discuss *two* specific problems caused by rapid industrialization, and explain how reformers sought to eliminate these problems.

PART A — SHORT ANSWER QUESTIONS

Directions: Analyze the documents and answer the question or questions that follow each document in the space provided. Your answers to the questions will help you write the essay.

> **NOTE:** On most D.B.Qs, there are 5 to 8 documents. At least two will be documents other than reading passages, such as cartoons or pictures. To simplify our explanation, this sample question has only four documents.

Document 1

> *"Old sausages that had been rejected and were moldy would be [sprayed] with glycerin and dumped into the hoppers for sale as sausages. In the factory, sausage meat would be used that had fallen on the floor, in the dirt and sawdust, where workers had spit their billions of germs. The meat was stored in rooms where water from leaky roofs would drip on it, and rats would race about on the piles of meat. It was too dark in the factory to see well, but a man could run his hand over the meat and sweep off handfuls of dried rat dung."*
>
> — Upton Sinclair, *The Jungle*, describing a meat-packing plant in 1906

1. According to Sinclair, what was the condition of the meat being prepared for sale as sausages? _____

_____

Document 2

> *"[Congress hereby] prohibits the manufacture, sale, or transportation of adulterated or misbranded or poisonous or deleterious [harmful] foods, drugs, medicines, and liquors."*
>
> — Pure Food and Drug Act of 1906

2. How did this law correct one of the abuses of rapid industrial growth? _____

_____

_____

Document 3

3. According to the photograph, what were conditions like for many children working in factories?

Museum of the City of New York

_____

_____

_____

Document 4

> *"Resolved: That we sympathize with the efforts of organized workingmen to shorten the hours of labor, eliminate the use of children in factories, and demand a rigid enforcement of the existing eight-hour law on work, and ask that a penalty clause be added to the said law."*
>
> — The Populist Platform of 1892

4a. What problems does this resolution in the Populist Platform identify? _____

_____

4b. How did the Populists seek to eliminate these abuses of rapid industrial growth?

_____

_____

_____

PART B — ESSAY

Directions:

Using information from the documents provided, and your knowledge of U.S. history, write a well-organized essay that includes an introduction, several paragraphs, and a conclusion.

Historical Context

Beginning in the 1890s, Americans set out to correct the problems caused by rapid industrial growth. Reformers worked to eliminate many of these abuses.

Task: Using information from the documents, and your knowledge of United States history, write an essay in which you:

> Discuss *two* specific problems caused by rapid industrialization, and explain how reformers sought to eliminate these problems.

Guidelines: Be sure to
- Address all aspects of the *Task* by analyzing and interpreting at least three documents
- Incorporate information from the documents in the body of the essay
- Incorporate relevant outside information throughout the essay
- Richly support the theme with relevant facts, examples, and details
- Write a well-developed essay that consistently demonstrates a logical and clear play of organization
- Introduce the theme by establishing a framework that is beyond a simple restatement of the *Task* or *Historical Context*, and conclude the essay with a summation of the theme.

USING THE L•A•W APPROACH

Notice how document-based questions have the following parts:

(1) directions on what to do
(2) a historical generalization that sets the stage for the essay question
(3) a task you must perform:
   - Part A, with up to eight documents to analyze; and
   - Part B, where you write the essay.

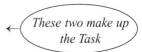
These two make up the Task

You need to focus on three areas: **(1)** **L**ook at the task; **(2)** **A**nalyze the documents; and **(3)** **W**rite the essay. To remember this approach, think of the word **LAW**.

"L" — LOOK AT THE TASK

Start by looking at the *Task*. Focus first on the question words. In this D.B.Q. the question words are *discuss* and *explain*. Then look at how many examples you must provide (two). Therefore, you must "discuss" *two* specific problems caused by rapid industrial growth, and "explain" how reformers sought to eliminate these problems. Your answers to the document questions will help you to organize and write the essay.

"A" — ANALYZE THE DOCUMENTS

Now you must focus on answering the question(s) following each document. Carefully answer all the questions in **Part A**. These answers will become the basis of the evidence you provide in your **Part B** essay. Take some time to examine each document. Notice how each question indicates what the testmakers want you to focus on in that document, in order to help you write your essay.

Next, you need a simple way to organize the information you provided in answering the **Part A** questions. A **Document Box** will be useful for this. The key to answering a D.B.Q. is to link the documents to the *Task*. In the Document Box, you show how information in the document supports your thesis statement. You also include additional information at the bottom of the box. Remember, the instructions specifically ask you to "incorporate relevant outside information throughout the essay."

Document	Main Ideas	Problem	Reform
Document 1: *(The Jungle)*	Conditions in meat-packing plant: reusing spoiled food, food picked off floor, leaky roof, rat droppings	Unsanitary food	
Document 2: (Pure Food Act)	Reacting to *The Jungle*, Congress passed food safety laws		Prohibited sale of harmful food and drugs
Document 3: (Photograph)	Two young girls working in factory at large textile machine	Child labor	
Document 4: (Populist Platform)	Fewer working hours, and an end to child labor		Shorter work day and no child labor

From your answers to the questions following the documents

Add relevant outside information

- Muckrakers drew attention to abuses of Big Business.
- Samuel Gompers formed the American Federation of Labor, a union that fought against child labor, long hours, low wages, poor working conditions.
- Progressives called for legislation to abolish child labor.

★ In the **Document** column, write a brief term to identify each document. The first document was a quote from *The Jungle*, so it is entered as Document 1.

★ In the **Main Ideas** column, describe in note form the main idea(s) of each document. The question following the document will often indicate what to focus on.

★ The final columns will depend on what you must cover in th[...] ample, you must discuss two problems and attempts to correct reform. This requires two additional columns: **Problem**, whe[...] two problems, and **Reform**, where you identify the reforms.

★ The directions tell you to include "relevant outside information." You [...] on your knowledge of U.S. history. The score of your answer will depend on [...] richly you support your thesis statement with facts, examples, and details.

"W" — WRITE THE ESSAY

In writing your essay answer, the key points to remember are:

★ **Introductory Paragraph (Top Bun)**. The opening sentence identifies the topic and sets the time and place. Remember, you acquire the topic from the *Task* statement, but state it in your own words. You must also state what you will show in your answer — this is your thesis statement. Then write a transition sentence that leads the reader from the introduction to your supporting paragraphs.

★ **Supporting Paragraphs (Patties of Meat)**. These paragraphs provide the details, facts and evidence to support your thesis statement. They must include references to at least three of the documents, as well as relevant outside information.

Discuss/Describe: This requires you to provide examples and details supporting your thesis statement.

Evaluate: To evaluate, you would write about the advantages and disadvantages. For example, if asked to *evaluate* the effects of rapid industrialization on American society, you might compare the advantages of producing vast amounts of goods at lower prices with the disadvantages of having young children working in factories and other abuses. Then make a final judgment about which was more important.

★ **Closing Paragraph (Bottom Bun)**. How you close the essay will depend on the question words in the *Task*. If the question asks you to *discuss* or *describe*, your conclusion should restate your thesis statement. For example, "Therefore, we can see that certain problems were caused by rapid industrial growth, and that reformers were successful in eliminating some of these problems." If the question asks you to *evaluate*, give the reader your final judgment. For example: "On balance, the benefits of industrialization outweighed the costs. Industrialization created a more productive society which provided cheaper and more plentiful goods, and the short-term abuses that resulted were gradually corrected."

CHAPTER 4

CONSTITUTIONAL FOUNDATIONS

In this chapter, you will learn how the thirteen English colonies formed an independent nation. The main challenge of this era was to create a democratic government strong enough to meet national needs without threatening its citizens' liberties. To meet this challenge, Americans drafted two documents — the Declaration of Independence and the U.S. Constitution. As you read this chapter, you will learn about:

National Archives

*The Declaration of Independence
being read in public for the first time*

- **From Colonies to Independent States**. American colonists objected to Britain's taxing them without their consent, setting off a conflict that led to the Revolutionary War. The Declaration of Independence asserted that the purpose of government was to meet the needs of the governed. Our first national government, under the Articles of Confederation, left most powers in the hands of the states. This system of government proved too weak to deal with the problems facing the new nation.

- **The Constitutional Convention**. The Constitution provided a strong government. Federalism, the separation of powers, and a system of checks and balances assured that no branch of government would have too much power. The first Congress then added a Bill of Rights to protect individual freedom.

- **Principles of the U.S. Constitution**. Our system of government is part of the legacy of the U.S. Constitution.

In studying this period, you should focus on the following questions:

✦ What were the basic ideas of the Declaration of Independence?
✦ How did the Constitution create a stronger central government without threatening individual liberties?
✦ Under the Constitution, how does our federal system of government work?

FROM COLONIES TO INDEPENDENT STATES

THE THIRTEEN ENGLISH COLONIES

By the 1730s, the Atlantic coastal plain from Georgia to New Hampshire had been divided into thirteen separate English colonies.

DEMOCRATIC TRADITIONS

The colonists enjoyed several democratic institutions, based in part on the English political tradition. In signing the **Magna Carta** of 1215, the English king had promised not to take away property or to imprison his nobles or townspeople except according to the laws of the land. The English had also developed a representative legislature, known as **Parliament**.

Other unique democratic traditions had developed among the colonists themselves. In 1620, Pilgrims crossing the Atlantic signed the **Mayflower Compact**, which established a colonial government deriving power from the consent of the governed. Virginia established its own **House of Burgesses**, in which elected representatives helped govern the colony. In fact, colonial assemblies came to act as lawmaking bodies throughout the

Pilgrims sign the Mayflower Compact

Library of Congress

colonies, ruling together with royal governors appointed in London. Because many people fled to the colonies to escape religious persecution, several colonies also developed a tradition of religious toleration.

THE SYSTEM OF MERCANTILISM

The American colonies grew in importance to Great Britain as their population and the value of their trade increased. Under **mercantilism**, trade with the colonies was regulated to benefit the "Mother Country" (*Great Britain*). The British sold expensive manufactured goods to the colonists, while the colonists sold cheaper raw materials, such as tobacco and cotton, to the British.

THE AMERICAN REVOLUTION, 1775-1783

In the mid-eighteenth century, Britain and France became involved in the **French and Indian War** (1754-1763). The British eventually defeated the French and gained control of Canada, but incurred a large debt in the course of the struggle.

"No Taxation without Representation"

To help pay off their war debt, the British Parliament imposed new taxes on the colonies. The **Stamp Act** (1765) required colonial newspapers, books and documents to carry an official government stamp. Colonists objected to the tax, since they were not represented in Parliament. After a wave of protests, Parliament repealed the tax, but replaced it with taxes on paper, glass and tea. The colonists again protested. The British finally repealed all these taxes except the one on tea. In 1773, a group of protesters threw tea off a British ship in Boston harbor. As a result of the **Boston Tea Party**, the British government closed

The Boston Tea Party

Library of Congress

Boston harbor and banned public meetings until the tea that had been destroyed was paid for. Representatives of the colonies met in Philadelphia to discuss the situation.

The Idea of Independence Grows

In 1775, British soldiers exchanged gunfire with colonial volunteers, marking the start of the American Revolution. As the fighting spread, many colonists began to argue for independence from Great Britain. In his pamphlet *Common Sense*, **Thomas Paine** wrote that it was ridiculous for the American colonies, located on a huge continent, to be governed by a tiny far-off island like Great Britain. Paine argued that it was only "common sense" for the colonists to seek independence.

The Declaration of Independence

In mid-1776, a committee headed by **Thomas Jefferson** drafted the Declaration of Independence. It was formally adopted by the **Second Continental Congress** in Philadelphia on **July 4, 1776**. The Declaration explained to the world why the colonists had declared independence from Britain. Its main ideas were taken from the "Social Contract" theory of **John Locke**. According to Locke, people form a government to protect their natural rights. If the government fails to protect its citizens and instead oppresses them, the citizens have a right to overthrow the government and create a new one. The Declaration stated that the colonists' rights had been violated, justifying their break with Great Britain.

General Washington accepts the surrender of the British at the end of the war

With help from the French, after years of fighting the Continental Army under General **George Washington** finally gained a hard-won victory over the British. In 1783, Britain recognized the independence of the thirteen American colonies. Each colony now became an independent state.

THE ARTICLES OF CONFEDERATION

Although each former colony enacted its own constitution, establishing thirteen separate state governments, Americans also recognized the need for some form of central government uniting all thirteen states.

THE FIRST NATIONAL GOVERNMENT

An agreement known as the **Articles of Confederation** went into effect in 1781, while the Revolutionary War was still being fought. The confederation was a weak, loose association of independent states. Each state sent one representative to the Confederation Congress, where it had one vote. There was no national executive or court. The Confederation Congress could not levy national taxes, regulate trade, or enforce its laws. Each state government was more powerful than the new national government.

ACCOMPLISHMENTS AND PROBLEMS

The Articles of Confederation held the nation together during the final years of the American Revolution. The Confederation Congress passed the **Northwest Ordinance** (1787), which provided a system for governing the western territories. Despite these successes, the period under the Articles is often called the **"Critical Period"** because of serious problems that arose. States taxed goods from other states, making trade between states difficult. Each state printed its own money, creating problems in selling goods between states. One of the most serious shortcomings of the national government was that after the Revolutionary War ended, it lacked the power to create a standing army.

THE NORTHWEST ORDINANCE OF 1787

CANADA (British)

LOUISIANA (Spanish)

NORTHWEST TERRITORY

DATES = YEAR ADMITTED TO THE UNION

In 1785, debtors and farmers in Massachusetts demanded cheap money to pay off their debts. **Shays' Rebellion** was put down by state troops, but if it had spread, the Confederation government would have been too weak to stop it. By 1786, merchants were unhappy that several states were obstructing trade. Property owners no longer felt safe. Many people feared that if a foreign country attacked the United States, the government would simply collapse. Several states called for a meeting to revise the Articles of Confederation.

THE CONSTITUTIONAL CONVENTION, 1787

Delegates from twelve states met in Philadelphia in 1787. They quickly decided to abandon the Articles of Confederation and to write a new **constitution** (*a document outlining the basic form and rules of government*). The delegates at the **Constitutional Convention** agreed on the need for a strong central government with a national executive, legislature, and judiciary.

A BUNDLE OF COMPROMISES

There were also important disagreements among the delegates, which were settled through a series of compromises.

- ✦ **The Great Compromise.** Large and small states differed on the method of representation for the new legislature. The Great Compromise resolved the conflict by creating a **bicameral** (*two-house*) Congress. In the **House of Representatives,** states would be represented according to the size of their population. In the **Senate,** each state would be represented by two Senators.

- ✦ **The Three-fifths Compromise.** Delegates from the South wanted to count slaves as part of a state's population, to increase their number of representatives in the House of Representatives. It was agreed that three-fifths of the slave population in a state would be counted for the purposes of representation and taxation.

- ✦ **The Slave Trade and Commerce Compromises.** Northern and Southern states differed over the slave trade and taxing exports. The delegates finally agreed that Congress would pass no laws restricting the slave trade for another twenty years (*until 1808*), and the new government would not have the power to tax exports.

THE DEBATE OVER RATIFICATION

A special convention was held in each state to ratify (*approve*) the Constitution. **Anti-Federalists** claimed the new Constitution created too powerful a government with no Bill of Rights to protect citizens' liberties. Leading **Federalists** like Alexander Hamilton argued in favor of the Constitution in *The Federalist Papers.* They claimed a stronger government was needed to protect against rebellion or foreign attack and to regulate interstate trade. They also said that citizens should not fear the new government, since its power was divided among three separate branches.

The signing of the Constitution, with George Washington presiding

By 1788, eleven states had ratified the Constitution. In 1789, the first Congress met in New York City. Later that month, George Washington stood on the balcony of Federal Hall in New York City and was inaugurated as the first President of the United States.

PRINCIPLES OF THE U.S. CONSTITUTION

The system of government established by the Constitution was based on several basic principles.

POPULAR SOVEREIGNTY

The most basic principle was that the final power in government is held by the people. This is reflected in the first words of the **Preamble**: "We, the people ..." Americans exercise this power by choosing their own representatives in democratic elections.

FEDERALISM

Federalism is a system for sharing power between the national and state governments. The federal (*national*) government deals with national matters and relations among the states, while state governments deal with matters within each state. **Concurrent powers**, such as the power to tax, are held by both the federal and state governments. **Reserved powers** are those held exclusively by state governments.

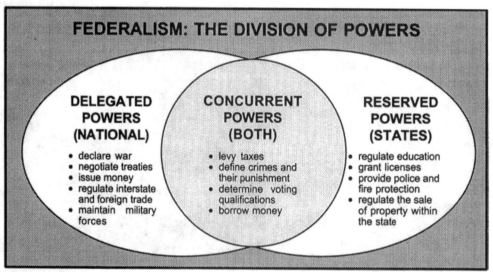

SEPARATION OF POWERS

To protect its citizens against tyranny, the national government's power was further divided among three branches: the Legislative, Executive, and Judicial branches. This separation of powers makes it almost impossible for any one individual or group to gain control of the entire government.

LIMITED GOVERNMENT

The Constitution strictly limits the power of federal and state government over our lives.

✦ **Delegated Powers.** The federal government has only those powers given to it by the Constitution. The Constitution also lists certain powers specifically denied to either the federal or state governments.

✦ **Implied Powers.** The **Elastic Clause** expands the powers of the federal government by giving Congress whatever additional powers are "necessary and proper" for carrying out those powers specifically listed in the Constitution. These additional powers are called the **implied powers**.

✦ **The Bill of Rights.** The Bill of Rights and later amendments to the Constitution placed additional limits on the powers of both our federal and state governments.

CHECKS AND BALANCES

To make sure that the national government did not become too strong or oppress those it was supposed to govern, the Constitution also gave each branch of the federal government several ways to stop or "check" the other branches.

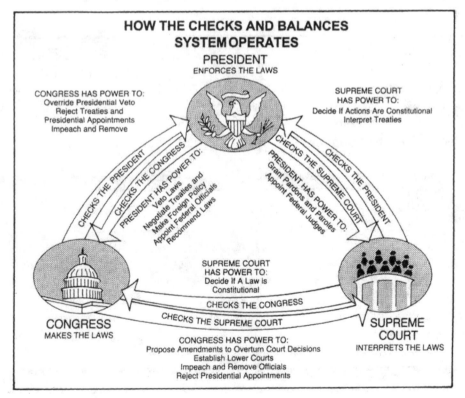

FLEXIBILITY

The Constitution is still in use today because it has the ability to adapt to changing situations through the amending process and new interpretations.

✦ **The Amending Process.** The Constitution can be changed by amendment. However, to prevent changes for unimportant reasons, the amending process was made much more difficult than the passage of an ordinary law. After Congress votes for a Constitutional amendment, three-quarters of the states must ratify it.

✦ **New Interpretations.** The Supreme Court has the job of interpreting the language of the Constitution. Its decisions often apply the Constitution to new circumstances. By finding new meaning, the Supreme Court helps adapt the text to the needs of the times.

THE UNWRITTEN CONSTITUTION

The federal government relies on many practices that developed after the Constitution was put into effect. These practices, often referred to as our "unwritten Constitution," became customary.

Cabinet
The Constitution gave the President power to appoint officials to assist him. Washington and later President relied on these officials — the Cabinet — for advice.

Political Parties
The Constitution did not specifically mention political parties, although these now play an essential role in our system of government.

THE "UNWRITTEN CONSTITUTION"

Judicial Review
The Supreme Court has the power to review federal and state laws to determine if they are **constitutional** (permitted under the Constitution).

Congressional Committees
These help Congress select the most important bills from the thousands proposed. Committees hold hearings and evaluate each bill.

THE FEDERAL GOVERNMENT: ITS STRUCTURE AND FUNCTIONS

Our federal government operates today with the same basic structure that the Constitution established more than two hundred years ago.

CONGRESS: THE LEGISLATIVE BRANCH

The main task of Congress is to make our nation's laws. It is composed of two houses both of which must approve any new law:

✦ **Senate.** The Senate has 100 members, two from each state. Each Senator is elected for a six-year term. In addition to its law-making function, two-thirds of the Senate is needed to ratify treaties negotiated by the President. The Senate must also confirm all Presidential appointments, such as nominees for federal judgeships, and ambassadors to foreign nations.

✦ **House of Representatives.** The House has 435 members. Each member is elected for a two-year term. The number of Representatives of each state is determined by that state's population. Every ten years a **census**

Members of the House of Representatives

is taken and the seats in the House of Representatives are redistributed.

THE PRESIDENCY: THE EXECUTIVE BRANCH

The President must be a natural-born citizen who is at least 35 years old. The President is elected for a four-year term. Traditionally, Presidents only served two terms of office, until Franklin D. Roosevelt was elected four times. In 1951, the **Twenty-second Amendment** was passed, limiting a President to two terms in office.

Choosing the President. The members of the Constitutional Convention did not trust the people to elect the President directly. Instead, they turned selection of the President to electors who form the **Electoral College**. To become President, a candidate needs to win a majority of the Electoral College votes. The number of electors each state has is equal to the number of its Representatives in the House combined with the number of its Senators. The candidate with the most votes in a state wins all of the electors of that state. If no candidate wins a majority of the Electoral College (270), the election must be decided by a special vote in the House of Representatives.

The Many Roles of the President. The Constitution defined the powers of the Presidency, but those powers have expanded since the Constitution was first adopted. Today, the President fills many roles — Chief Executive, Chief of State, Commander-in-Chief, foreign policy chief, chief legislator, and chief of a political party.

FEDERAL COURTS: THE JUDICIAL BRANCH

The **U.S. Supreme Court** is our highest federal court. The court has nine members, each nominated by the President and confirmed by the Senate. Below the Supreme Court are other federal courts, which try cases involving federal law or disputes between citizens from different states. Federal judges hold office for life, to protect their decisions from political interference. The Supreme Court can review lower-court decisions that come before it on appeal.

The chamber in which the U.S. Supreme Court hears cases

Judicial Review. In reviewing cases, the Supreme Court not only decides whether the law has been applied correctly, but also whether the law itself is within the power of the government according to the Constitution. The power of the Court to decide if laws are constitutional is known as **Judicial Review**. Chief Justice of the Supreme Court **John Marshall** (1801-1835) introduced judicial review and helped establish the importance of the federal judiciary and the supremacy of the national government over the states. His decisions helped foster a sense of national unity by expanding the federal government's power.

KEY DECISIONS OF THE MARSHALL COURT

- **Marbury v. Madison (1803)**. William Marbury asked the Supreme Court to require Secretary of State James Madison to deliver his commission (*an official appointment*), based on the Judiciary Act of 1789. The Court ruled that this part of the Judiciary Act was unconstitutional and that the Court had no power to order delivery of the commission. In so doing, the Court established the principle of judicial review, greatly strengthening the Supreme Court's authority as the final interpreter of the Constitution.

- **McCulloch v. Maryland** (1819). Maryland passed a law requiring the Maryland branch of the Bank of the United States to pay a state tax. Bank officials refused to pay. The Court ruled that a state could not tax an agency of the national government, such as the bank. The Court said that when a state law conflicts with a federal law, the federal law is supreme. The Court held that forming the national bank was constitutional. Although the Constitution did not specifically give Congress the power to create a bank, its creation was permissible under the "elastic clause."

PROTECTION OF INDIVIDUAL LIBERTIES

The first ten amendments, known as the **Bill of Rights,** were added to the Constitution in 1791. The Bill of Rights protects individuals only from actions of the federal government, but not from the actions of state governments.

The Bill of Rights

1st Amendment	Guarantees freedom of religion, speech, and the press, and the right to peacefully assemble and petition the government about grievances
2nd Amendment	Guarantees the right of citizens to keep and bear arms
3rd Amendment	Prohibits the quartering of soldiers in one's home
4th Amendment	Prohibits "unreasonable" searches and seizures by the government
5th Amendment	Contains guarantees and prohibitions that:no citizen may be deprived of life, liberty or property without **due process of law** (*procedures carried out according to rules, such as a fair trial*); requires **grand jury** indictments (*formal charge for committing a serious crime*); prohibits **double jeopardy** (*being tried twice for the same crime*); prohibits **self-incrimination** (*individuals may not be forced to give evidence against themselves*)
6th Amendment	Guarantees that those accused of a crime have the right to a speedy trial by jury, to confront accusers, and be represented by a lawyer
7th Amendment	Guarantees a jury trial in many civil cases
8th Amendment	Prohibits excessive bail and cruel and unusual punishment
9th Amendment	The listing of some rights does not mean that people do not have other rights
10th Amendment	Reserves to the states and the people all rights not given to the federal government

Several later amendments also contain important protections of individual rights. For example, the **Fourteenth Amendment** was especially important because it extended federal law to protect individuals from actions taken by state governments.

Other Amendments Protecting Individual Rights

13th Amendment	Prohibted slavery
14th Amendment	Gave former slaves citizenship, and guaranteed all citizens that they would enjoy "equal protection of the laws" and "due process of law" from state governments
15th Amendment	Guaranteed freed slaves the right to vote
17th Amendment	Changed the election of Senators from selection by state legislatures to direct election by voters
19th Amendment	Gave women the right to vote
24th Amendment	Prohibited poll taxes in federal elections
26th Amendment	Gave individuals the right to vote upon reaching age 18

CHECKING YOUR UNDERSTANDING

KEY TERMS AND CONCEPTS

Create a vocabulary card for each of the following terms and concepts:

- ◆ Declaration of Independence
- ◆ Articles of Confederation
- ◆ Bill of Rights
- ◆ Unwritten Constitution
- ◆ Federalism
- ◆ Judicial Review

MULTIPLE-CHOICE QUESTIONS

1   Which feature of government developed most fully during the colonial era?
1 separation of church and state
2 universal suffrage
3 equality under the law
4 representative assemblies

2   The primary purpose of the Declaration of Independence was to
1 establish the basic laws of the United States
2 justify to the world the revolt of the American colonists against Great Britain
3 provide a clear plan for a meaningful and effective political system
4 guarantee equal rights for all Americans

3 The Articles of Confederation created a
  1 republic with a chief executive
  2 strong central government
  3 national government with executive, legislative, and judicial branches
  4 league of loosely-organized independent states

4 At the Constitutional Convention of 1787, the "Great Compromise" resolved a dis-agreement concerning
  1 representation in Congress
  2 the future of slavery
  3 the powers of the Chief Executive
  4 control of interstate commerce

5 The basic purpose of our constitutional system of checks and balances is to
  1 protect states' rights
  2 prevent one branch of the government from becoming too powerful
  3 enable the federal government to run as efficiently as possible
  4 provide a written guarantee of the rights of each citizen

6 The U.S. government is considered a federal system because
  1 national laws must be passed by both houses of Congress
  2 powers are divided between the national and state governments
  3 the states are guaranteed a republican form of government
  4 the President is selected by the Electoral College

7 Which political development in the United States is considered part of the "unwritten constitution"?
  1 the system of checks and balances
  2 the formation of political parties
  3 the President's power to grant pardons
  4 the power of Congress to issue patents

8 The U.S. Supreme Court's decision in *Marbury v. Madison* was important because it
  1 defined the meaning of the Bill of Rights
  2 established the power of the Court to declare laws unconstitutional
  3 freed enslaved people in the South
  4 overturned the Commerce Clause of the U.S. Constitution

9   Which situation most clearly illustrates the principle of checks and balances?
    1 Congress listens to the President's State of the Union address.
    2 Congress votes on spending for the U.S. Navy
    3 The House of Representatives votes to impeach a federal judge.
    4 A Congressional committee revises the language of a bill.

10 The Supreme Court's power of judicial review is a result of
    1 an order by the President
    2 the Court's own interpretation of the Constitution
    3 a provision in the Bill of Rights
    4 the Court's decision to hear appeals regarding taxation

THEMATIC ESSAY QUESTION

Directions: Write a well-organized essay that includes an introduction, several paragraphs addressing the task, and a conclusion.

Theme: Constitutional Issues

> The Constitutional Convention of 1787 adopted several compromises to resolve disagreements over major issues facing the new nation.

Task:

> From your study of United States history, identify **two** issues from the Constitutional Convention of 1787.
>
> For *each* issue identified:
> • *Describe* the disagreement that arose over the issue at the Convention.
> • *Explain how* that issue was resolved through the use of compromise.

You may use any issue from your study of United States history. Some suggestions you might wish to consider include: representation in Congress, states' rights, slavery, tariffs, protection of civil liberties, and taxation.

You are *not* limited to these suggestions.

CHAPTER 5

THE CONSTITUTION TESTED

In this chapter, you will learn how the United States endured its first great test since independence — the American Civil War. After five years of fighting, the South lost the war. The Union was preserved and slavery came to an end. During the Reconstruction Era, Southerners struggled with the devastation of their social and economic systems, and developed new ways of life. As you read this chapter, you will learn about:

Library of Congress

After the Civil War, many cities lay in ruins

- **The Young Republic.** After independence, U.S. leaders expanded democracy, followed a policy of cautious neutrality toward Europe, and promoted westward expansion.

- **The Civil War.** When Abraham Lincoln was elected President, Southern states seceded from the U.S. The North's larger population, manufacturing facilities and greater naval power enabled it to win the war. During the conflict, Lincoln freed Southern slaves in the Emancipation Proclamation.

- **Reconstruction.** Southern states were only readmitted into the Union after they approved the 14th Amendment, protecting the rights of U.S. citizens from the acts of state governments. Congress imposed military rule on the South. After the end of Reconstruction, Southern states introduced racial segregation and denied African Americans the right to vote and other rights.

In studying this period, you should focus on the following questions:

✦ What were the goals of early American foreign policy?
✦ What were the causes of the Civil War?
✦ How did the South cope with the problems of Reconstruction?
✦ How did African Americans lose their rights following Reconstruction?

THE YOUNG REPUBLIC

LAUNCHING THE SHIP OF STATE

George Washington's Presidency (1789-1796) was especially significant because it laid the foundation for all later U.S. government.

❖ **The Cabinet**. To help carry out his duties, Washington appointed chief officers who met with him and the Vice President to form the **Cabinet**.

❖ **Hamilton's Financial Plan**. The new nation faced a large debt from the Revolutionary War. As Secretary of the Treasury, **Alexander Hamilton** proposed a program to put the nation's finances on a solid basis. He proposed that the federal government pay off the nation's debts, pass a high tariff to protect American industries, place a tax on whiskey, and create a national bank.

❖ **The Formation of Political Parties**. Thomas Jefferson and his followers believed Hamilton's plan favored the rich. They formed the nation's first political party, the **Democratic-Republicans**, to oppose the plan. Hamilton's supporters formed a second political party, the **Federalists**. The Federalists passed most of Hamilton's plan in Congress, except for the protective tariff.

PRESERVING AMERICAN INDEPENDENCE

After independence, American leaders adopted a policy of **neutrality** to avoid taking sides in European disputes. At the same time, they pursued a vigorous policy of westward expansion.

WASHINGTON'S FAREWELL ADDRESS (1796)

In his final address as President, George Washington cautioned against entering into a permanent alliance with any European country. Washington urged Americans to devote themselves to developing trade and influence in the Western Hemisphere.

THE LOUISIANA PURCHASE (1803)

In 1803, France offered to sell the Louisiana Territory to the United States for $15 million. Although Jefferson, who had become the nation's third President, was not sure if the Constitution allowed the federal government to buy territory, he went ahead with the purchase. The Louisiana Territory doubled the size of the United States.

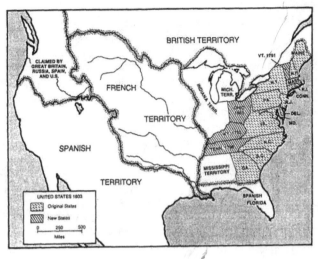

THE WAR OF 1812

To prevent the British seizure of American sailors in the Atlantic, to stop British support of Native American Indian raids in the Northwest Territory, and also to try to seize British Canada, Congress declared war on Britain in 1812. The war ended in a stalemate in 1815, coinciding with the end of the Napoleonic Wars in Europe.

THE MONROE DOCTRINE (1823)

Spain's attempts to restore its authority after the Napoleonic Wars triggered independence movements in its Latin American colonies. In the **Monroe Doctrine**, President Monroe announced that the U.S. would oppose any attempts by European powers to establish new colonies in the Western Hemisphere or to reconquer former colonies.

JACKSONIAN DEMOCRACY

Andrew Jackson was elected President in 1828. A native of Tennessee, Jackson was the first President not born to wealth and not from an Eastern state. His main supporters were ordinary people, especially laborers and Western frontiersmen.

AN AGE OF REFORM

Jackson's two terms in office saw an expansion of democracy. States eliminated property qualifications, allowing most adult males to vote. Selection of Presidential candidates by party leaders was replaced by nominating conventions. Jackson also developed the **spoils system**; supporters who helped in his election campaign replaced existing government officials. Jackson believed it was wise to change office-holders so that more people would have government experience. Jackson also forced the National Bank to close, since he believed it gave an unfair advantage to Eastern bankers and investors.

JACKSON AND THE NATIVE AMERICAN INDIANS

Under Jackson, Congress moved all remaining Native American Indians to territories west of the Mississippi River. Jackson refused to help the Cherokees of Georgia even though the Supreme Court declared that their forcible removal was unconstitutional.

MANIFEST DESTINY

In the 1840s, Americans began to believe it was their "manifest destiny," or future, to extend the nation's borders from the Atlantic to the Pacific Ocean.

❖ **Annexation of Texas, 1845**. American settlers in Texas declared their independence in 1835, when Mexico tried to prohibit further emigration from the United States. After a short war, Mexico recognized Texan independence. In 1845, Congress voted to annex Texas.

❖ **Mexican-American War, 1846-1848**. In 1846, war broke out between the U.S. and Mexico over the border of Texas. Mexico was quickly defeated and forced to give up California, Nevada, Utah, Arizona, and parts of Colorado and New Mexico.

❖ **Additional Acquisitions**. In 1853, the **Gadsden Purchase** from Mexico completed U.S. expansion in the southwest. In an agreement with Great Britain in 1846, the line dividing Canada and the United States was extended westward to the Pacific, giving the U.S. part of the **Oregon Territory**. In 1867, the United States purchased **Alaska** from Russia for $7.2 million.

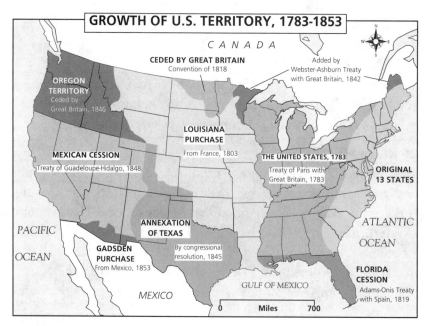

GROWTH OF U.S. TERRITORY, 1783-1853

THE CIVIL WAR, 1861-1865

CAUSES OF THE CIVIL WAR

A complex event like the American Civil War had many causes.

SECTIONALISM

By the early 19th century, each section of the country had developed its own special characteristics. These differences led to the rise of **sectionalism** — the greater loyalty many Americans felt towards their own particular section (*North, South or West*) than to the country as a whole.

SLAVERY

The most explosive issue facing the nation was slavery. **Abolitionists** wanted to end slavery. **Harriet Beecher Stowe's** book *Uncle Tom's Cabin* helped spread a sense of moral outrage against slavery in the North. Former slaves, such as **Frederick Douglass** and **Harriet Tubman**, were leading abolitionists. Pro-slave Southerners argued that slaves were better treated than Northern factory workers.

SLAVERY IN THE NEW TERRITORIES

The addition of new western territories posed the problem of whether an extension of slavery should be permitted. Southerners felt that extending slavery westward would preserve the balance between slave and free states in Congress. Northerners opposed the further spread of slavery. Between 1820 and 1850, national unity was preserved only by admitting new states in a series of compromises. In the 1850s, these compromises broke down. In 1854, Congress repealed the **Missouri Compromise** (1820) with the **Kansas-Nebraska Act**, which introduced popular sovereignty in the Kansas and Nebraska Territories. Then in 1857, in the case of *Dred Scott v. Sandford*, the Supreme Court ruled that Congress could not prohibit slavery in any U.S. territory.

STATES' RIGHTS

Southerners believed the Union was an agreement among states, and each state had the power to leave the Union if it wanted to. Northerners argued that the Constitution was the work of the American people, and that states had no right to leave the Union.

THE ELECTION OF LINCOLN

When Republican Presidential candidate **Abraham Lincoln** was elected in 1860, most Southern states **seceded** (*withdrew*) from the United States. The seceding states formed the **Confederate States of America**. Lincoln refused to recognize the secession of the South and resolved to preserve the unity of the United States.

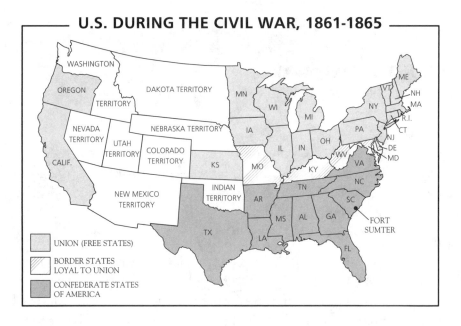

U.S. DURING THE CIVIL WAR, 1861-1865

UNION (FREE STATES)

BORDER STATES
LOYAL TO UNION

CONFEDERATE STATES
OF AMERICA

HIGHLIGHTS OF THE CIVIL WAR

Fighting broke out in 1861, when **Fort Sumter** was attacked by Confederate forces. The Confederacy hoped to win a quick victory and force the North to accept their independence. But the North had immense long-term advantages: a larger population, more money, more railroad lines, greater manufacturing facilities, and superior naval power. Despite these advantages, it took the North four years to defeat the South.

THE EMANCIPATION PROCLAMATION AND THE 13TH AMENDMENT

One of the most important events of the Civil War was the issuance of the **Emancipation Proclamation** (1862). Lincoln announced that all slaves in states still in rebellion on

Thousands of Union and Confederate soldiers were killed or wounded during the Civil War

Library of Congress

January 1, 1863 would be freed. The Proclamation gave a moral purpose to the war. However, it soon became unclear whether Lincoln had the constitutional power to free the slaves. Congress proposed the **Thirteenth Amendment**. When it was ratified in 1865, it abolished slavery throughout the United States.

THE RECONSTRUCTION ERA, 1865-1877

The **Reconstruction Era** after the Civil War was a time in which Americans faced the task of reunifying the nation and rebuilding the South.

RECONSTRUCTION

One major issue was how the Southern states were to be admitted back into the Union.

THE PRESIDENTIAL PLAN

President Lincoln believed the Southern states should be treated leniently. But only a few days after the South surrendered, Lincoln was assassinated. The new President, **Andrew Johnson**, sought to follow Lincoln's plan. Congress established the **Freedmen's Bureau** to help freed slaves (*known as freedmen*). However, Southern states passed **Black Codes** to preserve traditional Southern life-styles despite the ban on slavery. For example, the Black Codes made it illegal for freedmen to hold public office, travel freely or serve on juries.

Andrew Johnson

National Archives

THE CONGRESSIONAL PLAN

Northerners were outraged at the election of rebel leaders in the South and the passage of the Black Codes. Congress refused to recognize the new Southern governments. The **Radical Republicans**, a group of Northern Congressmen with a majority in Congress, wanted the freedmen to have political equality. The Radical Republicans passed a **Civil Rights Bill** guaranteeing freedmen's rights, and imposed military rule on the South. To ensure that this legislation would not be held unconstitutional, they rewrote the act as the **Fourteenth Amendment** — granting citizenship to all former slaves. The amendment also prohibited state governments from denying any citizen the right to a fair trial and equal protection under the law. Before being re-admitted into the Union, Southern states were required to ratify the amendment.

THE IMPEACHMENT OF PRESIDENT JOHNSON

President Andrew Johnson opposed the Congressional program. The Radical Republicans suspected Johnson, a Southerner from Tennessee, of being overly sympathetic to the South. Congress passed the **Tenure of Office Act**, limiting the President's power to dismiss his own Cabinet members. When Johnson dismissed his Secretary of War, the House of Representatives **impeached** (*indicted*) Johnson. In the Senate, the Radical Republicans fell just one vote short of convicting and removing him from office.

RECONSTRUCTION IN THE SOUTH

The **Fifteenth Amendment** guaranteed freedmen the right to vote. During Reconstruction, a new political leadership emerged in the South, consisting of **carpetbaggers** (*Northerners who went South to profit from Reconstruction*), **scalawags** (*Southern whites who had opposed the Confederacy*), and **freedmen**. Among the accomplishments of the Reconstruction governments were new public schools, laws banning racial discrimination, and the rebuilding of public roads, buildings, and railroads.

The first African-American Senator and Congressmen

THE AFTERMATH OF RECONSTRUCTION

In 1877, Reconstruction officially ended when the last remaining Northern troops were withdrawn from the South. Home rule was restored to Southern state governments. Former Confederate leaders could now serve in office. State legislatures quickly moved to bar African Americans from the political process.

THE ECONOMIC EFFECTS: THE NEW SOUTH

Without slave labor, the old plantation system could not be restored. Many plantation owners entered into share-cropping arrangements with their former slaves. Other freedmen became tenant farmers. Few freedmen were able to become landowners themselves. With financial backing from the North, railroads, cotton mills and furnaces for steel-making were built.

THE SOCIAL EFFECTS: THE SEGREGATED SOUTH

The social system that developed in the aftermath of Reconstruction was one of racial segregation and white supremacy, depriving African Americans of their political and civil rights. **Literacy tests** were introduced as a requirement for voting. Most freedmen lacked a formal education and could not pass these tests. **Poll taxes** were registration fees for voting, which many African Americans could not afford. **"Grandfather clauses"** allowed those whose ancestors had voted before the war to avoid passing a test or paying a tax to vote. These clauses empowered poor whites but not poor African Americans.

From the late 1800s through the 1950s, the Ku Klux Klan terrorized African Americans

Starting in the 1880s, Southern legislatures passed **"Jim Crow" laws** segregating African Americans from whites. African Americans were not permitted to ride in the same train cars, attend the same schools, or use any of the same public facilities as whites. In 1896, the Supreme Court upheld racial segregation in **Plessy v. Ferguson**.

AFRICAN-AMERICAN LEADERS SPEAK OUT

African-American leaders offered a variety of responses to these unjust conditions.

❖ **Booker T. Washington**, a former slave, believed that African Americans should concentrate on first trying to achieve economic independence before seeking full social equality. In 1881, he founded the Tuskegee Institute in Alabama.

❖ **W.E.B. DuBois** believed African Americans should work for full social equality immediately and not accept an inferior social and economic status. In 1909, DuBois helped form the **N.A.A.C.P.**, and began editing its journal, *The Crisis*.

Booker T. Washington

W.E.B. DuBois

CHECKING YOUR UNDERSTANDING

KEY TERMS, CONCEPTS, AND PEOPLE

- ✦ Monroe Doctrine
- ✦ Sectionalism
- ✦ Abolitionists
- ✦ Emancipation Proclamation
- ✦ "Jim Crow" laws
- ✦ Fourteenth Amendment
- ✦ *Plessy v. Ferguson*
- ✦ Booker T. Washington
- ✦ W.E.B. DuBois

MULTIPLE-CHOICE QUESTIONS

1 A fundamental reason for issuing the Monroe Doctrine (1823) was to
  1 halt the slave trade from Africa to the United States
  2 prevent European intervention in the Western Hemisphere
  3 prevent the start of the Civil War
  4 protect American interests in the Pacific

2 A supporter of Jacksonian democracy would have favored the idea of
  1 a government led by a king or queen
  2 a President selected by political party leaders
  3 the spoils system
  4 reduced military spending

3 The term "abolitionist" was used to describe a person who
  1 believed in free trade
  2 opposed foreign alliances
  3 wanted to end slavery
  4 supported colonial rule

4 The decision in *Dred Scott v. Sandford* (1857) was important because it
  1 strengthened the determination of abolitionists to achieve their goals
  2 triggered the immediate outbreak of the Civil War
  3 ended the importation of slaves into the United States
  4 increased the power of Congress to exclude slavery from new territories

5 Which best explains Lincoln's decision to engage in the Civil War?
  1 As an abolitionist, Lincoln wanted to end slavery.
  2 Lincoln wanted to keep the South dependent on the industrial North.
  3 Lincoln's oath of office required him to defend and preserve the Union.
  4 Lincoln wanted to protect the freedom of the seas.

6 Which was a major result of the Civil War?
  1 Slavery was ended.
  2 The U.S. won independence.
  3 States secured the right to secede.
  4 Women gained the right to vote.

7 Radical Republicans opposed Lincoln's Reconstruction plan because it
   1 demanded payments from the South that would damage its economy
   2 postponed readmission of Southern states into the Union for many years
   3 granted too many rights to formerly enslaved people
   4 allowed the election of Confederate leaders in the South

8 How were African Americans in the South affected by the end of Reconstruction?
   1 A constitutional amendment guaranteed their social advancement.
   2 The Freedmen's Bureau helped them become independent farm owners.
   3 "Jim Crow" laws introduced racial segregation.
   4 Southern landowners offered them new voting rights.

9 Booker T. Washington disagreed with the ideas of W.E.B. Du Bois in that Washington believed African Americans should
   1 first concentrate on achieving economic independence
   2 use violence to achieve their goals
   3 initially focus on achieving full social equality
   4 remain in the South

THEMATIC ESSAY QUESTION

Directions: Write a well-organized essay that includes an introduction, several paragraphs addressing the task, and a conclusion.

Theme: Controversies in American History

> Throughout American history, individuals and groups have often disagreed about certain controversial issues.

Task:

> From your study of U.S. history, identify **two** controversies.
> For *each* controversy identified:
> - *Describe* the circumstances surrounding the controversy.
> - *Explain* how the controversy was resolved or settled.

You may use any examples from your study of U. S. history and government. Some suggestions you might wish to consider include: large states vs. small states at the Constitutional Convention, Thomas Jefferson vs. Alexander Hamilton over Hamilton's financial plan, Northern states vs. Southern states over slavery, Andrew Johnson vs. the Radical Republicans over plans for Reconstruction, and Booker T. Washington vs. W.E.B. DuBois over the best strategy for African Americans.

You are *not* limited to these suggestions.

DOCUMENT-BASED ESSAY QUESTION

This question is based on the accompanying documents (1-5). This question is designed to test your ability to work with historical documents. Some of the documents have been edited for the purposes of the question. As you analyze the documents, take into account both the source of each document and any point of view that may be presented in the document.

Historical Context: Soon after the Civil War, constitutional amendments were passed to provide African Americans with freedom and equality. However, during the century that followed, most African Americans still lacked real equality.

Task: Using information from the documents and your knowledge of U.S. history, answer the questions that follow each document in Part A. Your answers to the questions will help you write the Part B essay, in which you will be asked to:

> Describe the treatment of African Americans in the South in the century following the Civil War.

Part A — Short Answer Questions

Directions: Analyze the documents and answer the questions that follow each document in the space provided. Your answers will help you write the essay.

Document 1:

"Neither slavery nor involuntary servitude, except as a punishment for crime...shall exist within the United States, or any place subject to their jurisdiction."
                                                          — *13th Amendment (1865)*

"All persons born or naturalized in the United States, and subject to the jurisdiction thereof, are citizens of the United States and of the state wherein they reside. No state shall make or enforce any law which shall abridge the privileges and immunities of citizens of the United States, nor shall any state deprive any person of life, liberty or property without due process of law."
                                           — *14th Amendment, Section 1 (1868)*

"The right of the citizens of the United States to vote shall not be denied or abridged by the United States or by any state, on account of race, color, or previous condition of servitude."
                                           — *15th Amendment, Section 1 (1870)*

1. What rights did African Americans gain, based on these amendments?_____

Document 2:

BARRIER	DESCRIPTION
Poll Tax	A voting tax that discriminated against poor people by requiring a person to pay a fee in order to vote.
Property Test	A requirement that a person must own a certain amount of property to vote; a requirement few poor Americans could meet.
Literacy Test	A requirement that a person must be able to read to vote; white registrars decided who had passed the test.
Grandfather Clauses	These clauses waived literacy and property tests only for those whose grandfather had been eligible to vote before the Civil War.
Primary Elections	African Americans were barred from voting in primaries, since such elections were not covered by the 15th Amendment.

2. What impact did these barriers have on African-American voting? _____

Document 3:   SELECTED "JIM CROW" LAWS, 1870-1935

Date	State	Purpose of Law	Date	State	Purpose of Law
1870	Georgia	segregated schools	1906	Alabama	segregated streetcars
1900	S. Carolina	segregated railroad cars	1915	S. Carolina	unequal spending for education
1905	Georgia	segregated parks	1922	Mississippi	segregated taxicabs

3. What impact did "Jim Crow" laws have on Southern society? _____

Document 4:

"I am a member of this honorable body. Yet, when I come to the capital to make laws for this Republic, I am treated not as an American citizen, but as a brute. Forced to occupy a filthy smoking-car, with drunkards, gamblers and criminals; and for what? Simply because I have a darker complexion. If this treatment was confined to persons of our own sex we could possibly endure it. But our wives, daughters, sisters and mothers are subjected to the same insults and uncivilized treatment. The only time I ever question my loyalty to my government is when I leave my home to go traveling."

— *John Lynch of Mississippi, member of the House of Representatives, 1870-1876*

4. Why did John Lynch feel that he was being treated "as a brute?"_____

Document 5:

5. What does this photograph tell us about how African Americans were treated in the South in the early 1900s?

Library of Congress

_____

_____

_____

Part B — Essay

Directions:
- Write a well-organized essay that includes an introduction, several paragraphs, and a conclusion.
- Use evidence from at least **three** documents to support your response.
- Include additional related information.

Historical Context:
Soon after the Civil War, amendments were passed to provide African Americans with freedom and equality. However, during the century that followed, most African Americans still lacked real equality.

Task:
Using information from the documents and your knowledge of United States history, write an essay in which you:

> Describe the treatment of African Americans in the South in the century following the Civil War.

ANSWERING A DOCUMENT-BASED QUESTION

Let's use the "L • A • W" approach you learned about in Chapter 3.

"L" — LOOK AT THE TASK
Start by looking at the *Historical Context* and the *Task* requirements. In looking at the *Task*, focus on the "question word" and the topic of the question.

"A" — ANALYZE THE DOCUMENTS

Remember that the answers you provide to the questions in **Part A** will greatly help you to write the **Part B** essay. Therefore, make sure that you refer to your answers to the document questions in completing your **Document Box**. Information about the first document and some relevant outside information have been provided for you, to help you get started. Complete the rest of the **Document Box** for the other documents. Remember, when analyzing a document, relate it to the *Task*.

— DOCUMENT BOX —

Document	What the document says about the treatment of African Americans following the Civil War
Document 1: (Civil War Amendments)	*The Civil War Amendments promised African Americans (1) freedom from slavery, (2) the right to vote, (3) rights and privileges of U.S. citizens.*
Document 2: (Barriers to Voting)	*[You should complete]*
Document 3: (Jim Crow Laws)	*[You should complete]*
Document 4: (Congressman)	*[You should complete]*
Document 5: (Photograph)	*[You should complete]*

← Analyze these documents

Relevant outside information:
- *After Civil War, many freedmen became sharecroppers or tenant farmers on white-owned lands*
- *Supreme Court upheld racial segregation in Plessy v. Ferguson (1896)*
- _____
- _____

←Add relevant information

"W" — WRITE THE ANSWER

Now that you have looked over the *Task* and analyzed the documents, you are ready to write your essay. Use the following page to write your answer. Some of the essay has already been written for you. Complete the rest of the essay using information in your **Document Box** as a guide.

① The Introduction →

Just after the Civil War, the Civil War Amendments — the Thirteenth, Fourteenth, and Fifteenth Amendments shown in Document 1 — were passed to provide African Americans with freedom and equality. However, during the century that followed the passage of these amendments, African Americans found that they had achieved freedom without real equality. Following the end of Reconstruction, white Southerners moved to place limits on African Americans in order to preserve their control over Southern society.

② The topic of this paragraph is the denial of voting rights. Notice the reference to Document 2. →

One of the most important steps Southern states took was to pass a variety of laws to prevent African Americans from voting. As shown in Document 2, since African Americans could not pass literacy tests or pay poll taxes, they could not vote. This ensured white political control. African Americans were given the message that, despite the Civil War Amendments, they were not full citizens. Without political or economic power, African Americans had limited ability to improve their conditions or to promote change.

③ The rest of your essay should furthur describe the treatment of African Americans in the South. →

_____

_____

_____

_____

_____

_____

_____

_____

_____

_____

④ Your conclusion →

Therefore, although the Civil War Amendments promised African Americans freedom and equality, the century following the passage of these amendments saw most African Americans achieve only limited freedom without real equality.

CHAPTER 6

THE RISE
OF INDUSTRY

In this chapter, you will learn how the United States became one of the world's leading industrial powers in the decades following the Civil War (1865-1900). A revolution of new ideas and inventions transformed the nation. Industrialization proceeded at an explosive pace, bringing with it enormous changes that affected nearly every aspect of American life. It is helpful to think of these changes as occurring in the following areas:

In the late 1800s, immigrants entered the United States in ever-increasing numbers

- **The Rise of American Industry.** The development of new machines led to the rise of factories and mass production. Population growth, immigration and railroad expansion led to the rise of a national market. Entrepreneurs like Andrew Carnegie and John D. Rockefeller helped spearhead these changes.

- **The Rise of Labor.** Often ill-treated and poorly paid, industrial workers organized into unions to obtain better working conditions. At first, public opinion opposed unions, but attitudes changed in the early 20th century.

- **Urbanization and Immigration.** People flooded into cities in search of jobs and a better life. Immigrants were also attracted to cities. Cities grew so rapidly they could not deal with the problems of overcrowding and insufficient public services.

- **The Last Frontier.** The completion of transcontinental railroads allowed settlers to occupy the Great Plains and Far West. Native American Indian tribes were forced onto reservations by the U.S. government.

In studying this period, you should focus on the following questions:

✦ What forces enabled the United States to emerge as a leading industrial power?
✦ How were workers affected by the rise of industry?
✦ How did cities cope with new problems?
✦ What factors led to increasing immigration to the United States?

THE RISE OF AMERICAN INDUSTRY

The **Industrial Revolution** began in Great Britain in the mid-1700s, and reached the United States in the early 1800s. New inventions and ideas introduced new ways of making goods and meeting people's needs. Instead of producing goods by hand at home, people worked in factories. Water power or steam engines powered the machines in these factories, allowing manufacturers to produce more goods for less money. As goods became cheaper, demand increased, creating more jobs. Cities grew as people moved into them in order to find work.

Ford Motor Company

As industry grew, scenes like this at a Ford factory became typical around the nation

THE MODERN INDUSTRIAL ECONOMY EMERGES

American industrialization proceeded at an increased pace after the Civil War.

THE EXPANSION OF RAILROADS

The first transcontinental railroad, linking the east and west coasts, was completed in 1869. Railroads connected raw materials to factories and factories to consumers throughout the nation. Construction of the railroads stimulated the iron, steel and coal industries. It also played a key role in the settlement of the West.

THE GROWTH OF POPULATION

Between 1860 and 1900, the population of the United States more than doubled. This population increase was partly fueled by a constant stream of European immigrants. Population growth created favorable conditions for business expansion — a steadily rising demand for goods and a source of cheap labor.

DEVELOPMENT OF A NATIONAL MARKET

In the late 19th century, a national market developed as a result of a number of factors. Railroads, telegraphs and telephones linked different parts of the country. National producers could make and ship goods more cheaply than local producers.

TECHNOLOGICAL PROGRESS

New technologies helped fuel the economic expansion of the late 19th century. The **Bessemer process** made steel production more economical. By 1900, **Thomas Edison**'s expanded uses for electricity powered an increasing number of machines, including electric streetcars and subway trains. The internal combustion engine, developed at the end of the 19th century, was used to run cars and the first airplanes. Each major new invention had a dramatic effect on the American economy.

SOME IMPORTANT INVENTIONS AND INNOVATIONS	
Elias Howe: **sewing machine (1846)**	Alexander Graham Bell: **telephone (1876)**
Elisha Otis: **passenger elevator (1852)**	Thomas A. Edison: **electric light bulb (1879)**
Christopher Sholes: **typewriter (1867)**	Orville and Wilbur Wright: **airplane (1903)**

NEW FORMS OF BUSINESS ORGANIZATION

Following the Civil War, the corporate form of business became more popular. A **corporation** is a company that issues shares to investors, making each **stockholder** a partial owner. Stockholders share in a corporation's profits in the form of dividends. Corporations became widespread because of the large amounts of money they could raise.

ENTREPRENEURSHIP

Those who brought these new factors together to create large businesses also played a crucial role in the rise of industry. Because of the lavish lifestyle of those who became rich from industry, the period from 1865 to 1900 became known as the **Gilded Age**. Through the efficiencies of large-scale production, these industrialists lowered the prices of goods, making them more affordable. But some called these entrepreneurs **robber barons** because of the ruthless tactics they used to destroy competition and to keep down workers' wages. Two of the most famous entrepreneurs were:

✦ **Andrew Carnegie** (1835-1919) worked his way up from a penniless Scottish immigrant to become one of America's richest men. His steel mills ruthlessly undercut all competition. His workers put in 12-hour shifts at low wages. Carnegie hired thugs to crush any worker attempts to unionize.

✦ **John D. Rockefeller** (1839-1937) formed the **Standard Oil Company** in 1870. Rockefeller forced railroad companies to give him special, secret rates for shipping his oil, while they charged his competitors higher prices.

BIG BUSINESS CONSOLIDATION

Beginning with the **Depression of 1873**, many large producers like Carnegie and Rockefeller began driving smaller companies out of business or acquiring them. In other cases, rival companies reached agreements to consolidate (*join together*), often in **trusts**. Many producers hoped to eliminate competition by establishing a **monopoly** (*complete control of the manufacture of a product*). Monopolistic power allowed them to dictate their own prices to consumers.

THE DEMAND FOR REFORM GROWS

At first, U.S. leaders believed that government should not interfere in the operation of the free market. However, some abuses of big business were so glaring that reformers called for federal laws to remedy them. As a result, new legislation was passed:

✦ **Interstate Commerce Act** (1887) was enacted when the Supreme Court overruled state laws regulating railroads. This new federal law prohibited unfair practices by railroads, such as charging more money for shorter routes.

✦ **Sherman Anti-Trust Act** (1890) was passed to check the spread of monopolies. It outlawed unfair monopolistic practices that stifled competition.

THE RISE OF ORGANIZED LABOR

One factor in America's rapid economic growth was an increasing exploitation of industrial workers. Gains in increased industrial productivity and higher corporate profits were often achieved at a terrible human cost.

INDUSTRIAL WORKERS FACE NEW PROBLEMS

Industrial working conditions in the late 19th century were often quite hazardous. Safeguards around machinery were inadequate. Thousands of workers were injured or killed in accidents each year. Workers faced a six-day work week of 10 to 14 hours per day. Pay averaged from $3 to $12 weekly. Jobs were on a take-it or leave-it basis. Usually a worker had no choice but to accept. Industrial workers could be fired for any reason. There was no unemployment insurance, worker's compensation, health insurance or old-age insurance.

About one in five children under the age of 15 worked in 1910

Library of Congress

RISE OF LABOR UNIONS

With the rise of big business, individual workers lost all bargaining power with their employers. Many workers realized that some form of labor organization was needed to protect their interests. They formed **unions** so that they could act as a group. Unions organized strikes and other forms of protest to obtain better working conditions. Industrialists like Carnegie used immigrant workers or closed down factories rather than negotiate with unions.

WORKERS SEEK A NATIONAL VOICE

The Knights of Labor, begun in 1869, hoped to form one large national union joining together all skilled and unskilled workers. Under the leadership of **Terrence Powderly**, the Knights of Labor grew rapidly in the prosperous times of the 1880s. But the Knights proved to be too loosely organized to be effective against the power of large companies. After losing several important strikes, the Knights of Labor fell apart.

These workers, laying railroad track, labored long hours for very low wages

Library of Congress

THE AMERICAN FEDERATION OF LABOR

The American Federation of Labor (AFL) was formed in 1881 by **Samuel Gompers**. Gompers hoped to create a powerful union by uniting workers with similar economic interests. Unlike the Knights of Labor, the AFL consisted of separate unions of skilled workers joined together into a federation. Gompers limited his goals to winning improved wages and working conditions for workers, higher pay, and an 8-hour work day. Gompers fought hard to improve members' job security by seeking **closed shops** (*places where only union members were hired*). The AFL quickly emerged as the principal voice of organized labor.

GOVERNMENT'S ATTITUDE TOWARD UNIONS

In the late 19th century, most government leaders favored business and opposed unions.

REASONS WHY GOVERNMENT FAVORED BUSINESS

Unions lacked political strength, while business leaders contributed heavily to political campaigns. Moreover, business leaders and politicians often shared the same outlook — that businessmen, not workers, were responsible for creating prosperity. Public opinion also favored *laissez-faire* policies, believing businesses should have the right to hire and fire employees as they pleased. Finally, union activities were often associated with violence. In the **Haymarket Affair** of 1886, labor leaders were blamed when a bomb exploded at a demonstration of striking workers at Haymarket Square in Chicago.

A SHIFT IN GOVERNMENT ATTITUDE

In the early 20th century, the attitude of the government and public towards unions began to change. One event that caused this change was a fire at the **Triangle Shirtwaist Factory** in 1911. Almost 150 young women workers died because the factory doors had been bolted shut from the outside. Soon after, Congress passed legislation favorable to unions. Congress also created the **Department of Labor** to study labor problems, collect statistics, and enforce labor laws. Congress also passed a law to prevent applying antitrust laws to unions. The **Clayton Antitrust Act** banned the use of federal **injunctions** (*court orders*) to prohibit strikes in labor disputes.

URBANIZATION

One important result of industrialization was the rapid expansion of American cities.

The movement of people from rural areas to cities is known as **urbanization**. Cities grew so quickly that municipal authorities could not deal with their problems. Large families crowded into **tenements** — single-room apartments often without heat or lighting. Many families had to share a single toilet. Horse-drawn carts crammed the streets. Factories polluted the air, and sewage contaminated drinking water. Cities were unable to deliver many essential services, such as sufficient police, schools, and garbage collec-

Typical urban congestion in 1900

New York State Archives

tion. Cities were often run by corrupt "**political machines**." Political bosses provided jobs and services for immigrants and the poor in exchange for their votes. The bosses used their control of city hall to make illegal profits on city contracts.

IMMIGRATION

Late 19th century America experienced a sudden flood of immigrants. Up until 1880, most immigrants had come from Northern Europe. In general, these **"Old Immigrants"** were Protestant, except for Irish Catholics, and most spoke English. Immigration patterns changed in the 1880s. Railroads and steamships made the voyage to America more affordable. Most

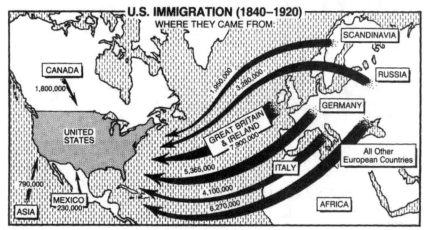

"New Immigrants" came from Southern and Eastern Europe, especially Poland, Italy, Austria-Hungary, Greece, and Russia. They were Catholic and Jewish, spoke no English, were poor, and dressed differently from Northern Europeans. A trickle of Asian immigrants also arrived.

THE PROCESS OF BECOMING AMERICANIZED

The New Immigrants often settled in cities. They were unfamiliar with American customs, lived in crowded apartments, and worked as unskilled laborers for long hours at low pay. They often faced hostility and discrimination from native-born Americans and from other ethnic groups. Many of the New Immigrants settled with others of the same nationality in neighborhoods known as **ghettos**. However, this isolated them from mainstream American life. While some attended night school to learn English, most were too busy working or caring for families to learn a new language or culture. It was left to their children to learn English and become familiar with American customs. In this way, immigrant children were eventually **assimilated** or **"Americanized."**

THE RISE OF NATIVISM

As the flood of immigrants grew at the end of the 1800s, nativist hostility mounted. Nativists called for restricted immigration. They argued that New Immigrants were inferior to "true" Americans — white, Anglo-Saxon and Protestant. Nativists believed that people of other races, religions and nationalities were physically and culturally inferior.

RESTRICTIONS ON IMMIGRATION

In the late 1800s, the first acts restricting immigration were passed. The **Chinese Exclusion Act** (1882) was passed to pacify anti-Chinese feelings in California against the flood of Chinese workers: all Chinese immigration was banned. In the **Gentlemen's Agreement** (1907), the Japanese government promised to limit future Japanese immigration. Restrictions on immigration from Eastern and Southern Europe were introduced in the 1920s.

THE LAST FRONTIER

The American **frontier** is generally defined as the line separating areas of settlement from "unsettled" wilderness and Native American Indian territory. Since the first colonists arrived, the frontier had moved gradually westwards. By the end of the Civil War, settlers occupied the Midwestern prairies and had a foothold along the Pacific coast.

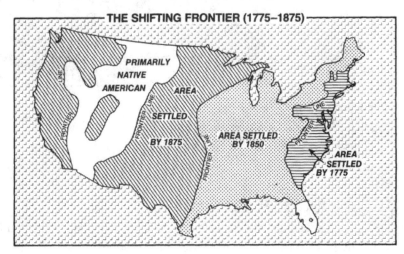

THE SHIFTING FRONTIER (1775–1875)

Between these two lines remained a vast expanse of territory.

SETTLEMENT OF THE LAST FRONTIER

Much of this last frontier consisted of the Great Plains, home to millions of buffalo and the Native American Indian tribes who lived off their meat and hides. From 1860 to 1890, the herds of buffalo were destroyed, and tribes were forced onto reservations. The Great Plains were then divided into farms and ranches.

THE DISCOVERY OF PRECIOUS METALS

Gold and silver were discovered in California, the Rocky Mountains and the Black Hills of North Dakota from 1848 onwards. Thousands of prospectors and adventurers moved to these areas in the hope of striking it rich.

THE ROLE OF THE RAILROADS

The extension of the railroads, especially after completion of the transcontinental railroad in 1869, was the principal factor in the settlement of the Great Plains. Railroads made it possible for ranchers and farmers to ship cattle and grain to eastern markets.

THE AVAILABILITY OF CHEAP LAND

Immigrants from Europe and farmers from the East and Midwest were attracted by the prospect of cheap land under the terms of the **Homestead Act** (1862), which gave federal land away to anyone who would live on the land and farm it for five years.

THE FATE OF THE NATIVE AMERICAN INDIANS

From 1830 to 1890, federal and state governments followed a policy of pushing Native American Indians from their traditional lands onto government reservations in the West. The "**Indian Wars**," which pitted settlers and federal troops against the tribes, lasted from 1860 to 1890. **Reservations** were often smaller than the lands from which the tribe was removed, and frequently consisted of undesirable land. The federal government promised food, blankets and seed, but this policy often clashed with tribal customs, since Native American Indians were traditionally hunters, not farmers.

REFORMERS URGE AMERICANIZATION

In the 19th century, prejudice against Native American Indians was widespread. Nonetheless, some reformers began to protest their mistreatment. The most famous of these was **Helen Hunt Jackson**. Her book *A Century of Dishonor* (1881) harshly criticized the government for repeatedly breaking its promises to Native American Indians.

THE DAWES ACT, 1887

Many reformers urged that Native American Indian tribes adopt the culture of most Americans. The **Dawes Act** sought to hasten their Americanization. The act officially abolished Native American Indian tribes. Each family was given 160 acres of reservation land as its own private property. Although well-intentioned, the Dawes Act was a failure. It did not take into account such traditions as tribal ownership, and the government never provided all the support it had promised.

CHECKING YOUR UNDERSTANDING

KEY TERMS, CONCEPTS, AND PEOPLE

- ✦ Gilded Age
- ✦ Andrew Carnegie
- ✦ Urbanization
- ✦ New Immigrants
- ✦ Gentleman's Agreement
- ✦ Nativism
- ✦ Reservations
- ✦ Helen Hunt Jackson
- ✦ Dawes Act

MULTIPLE-CHOICE QUESTIONS

1   A major cause of industrialization in the United States was the
    1 Fourteenth Amendment   3 development of labor unions
    2 Sherman Anti-Trust Act   4 expansion of railroads

2   Which statement about the Sherman Anti-Trust Act (1890) is most accurate?
    1 It gave states the power to regulate interstate railways.
    2 It prohibited monopolies that restricted interstate commerce.
    3 It established the Federal Trade Commission.
    4 The Supreme Court ruled that it was unconstitutional.

3   The term "Gilded Age" suggests that in the latter part of the nineteenth century, many
    Americans were concerned with
    1 materialistic goals   3 overseas expansion
    2 social equality   4 artistic achievement

4   What was the greatest problem facing American industrial workers in the late
    nineteenth century?
    1 shortage of farm crops   3 decreased rates charged by railroads
    2 inability to vote in elections 4 harsh working conditions

5   Which was a major reason for the failure of 19th century labor unions?
    1 public disapproval of unions
    2 Congressional measures outlawing unions
    3 an abundance of technical workers
    4 a general satisfaction among workers with their working conditions

6   Which belief was shared by the Knights of Labor and the American Federation of
    Labor?
    1 To become strong, unions must limit their membership.
    2 Unskilled workers should be excluded from union membership.
    3 Union membership should be open to corporate managers.
    4 Unions should represent the voice of workers.

7   Which statement about immigration to the United States is most accurate?
    1 Industrialization reduced the demand for cheap immigrant labor.
    2 Immigrants helped to create a low-cost source of labor.
    3 Organized labor generally favored unrestricted immigration.
    4 Most immigration legislation was passed to encourage immigration.

8 Which was an important effect of the Homestead Act of 1862?
1 Chinese immigration to California was restricted.
2 Railroads stopped charging excessive rates on local routes.
3 Native American Indian families obtained their own lands to farm.
4 Settlers obtained ownership of the federal lands they farmed.

9 A common complaint of Nativist groups during the late 19th century was that
1 Congress failed to protect domestic industries.
2 Many immigrants had customs and beliefs that were "un-American."
3 Too many elected officials came from rural backgrounds.
4 Native American Indians should be given back some of their ancestral lands.

10 After the Civil War, the policy of the U.S. government toward Native American Indians was mainly one of
1 moving them from ancestral lands onto government-designated reservations
2 encouraging them to retain their customs and traditions
3 educating society about their cultural heritage
4 shifting responsibility for Native American Indian affairs to state governments

THEMATIC ESSAY QUESTION

Theme: Economic Changes

> At various periods in United States history, groups of people have been profoundly influenced by economic changes.

Task:

From your study of United States history, identify **two** groups.

For *each* group identified:
- *Describe* the role that group played in the American economy.
- *Identify* an action or event that affected that group.
- *Discuss* how the condition of the group changed after that action or event.

You may use any examples from your study of United States history. Some suggestions you might consider include: Native American Indians (1865-present), factory workers (1865-1920), entrepreneurs (1865-1920), immigrants (1890-1920), farmers (1929-present), and city-dwellers (1880-1940).

You are *not* limited to these suggestions.

CHAPTER 7

THE PROGRESSIVE ERA: PROTEST, REFORM, AND EMPIRE

In this chapter, you will learn how Americans adopted important reforms to meet the new problems posed by industrialization and urbanization. American industrial power also enabled the nation to become a world power. As the nation grew more assertive, it acquired its first overseas colonies. In this chapter you should be aware of the following:

In these years, women became more vocal in their demand for the right to vote

- **Agrarian Reform and Populism.** In the late nineteenth century, farmers were harmed by falling food prices while their expenses remained high. To protect themselves, American farmers organized to demand change.

- **Progressive Movement.** Progressive reformers sought to end political corruption, to curb the abuses of big business, and to remedy the social problems caused by industrialization. Presidents Theodore Roosevelt and Woodrow Wilson introduced Progressive reforms at the national level.

- **Struggle for Women's Rights.** American women organized amd became more forceful in their attempts to achieve equal rights with men.

- **American Foreign Policy, 1898-1920.** Americans went to war with Spain in 1898 to halt atrocities in Cuba. After the war, the U.S. acquired a colonial empire. In 1917, the nation was drawn into World War I in Europe.

In studying this period, you should focus on the following questions:

✦ What were the problems of farmers and how did they try to overcome them?
✦ What changes were brought about by the Progressives?
✦ What changes took place in the lives of American women?
✦ Why did the United States become involved in World War I?

AGRARIAN REFORM AND POPULISM

THE AGRARIAN MOVEMENT

In the late nineteenth century, farmers experienced increasing difficulties:

REASONS FOR FARMERS' ECONOMIC PROBLEMS

Overproduction. The opening of the West increased the amount of farmland. Machinery raised productivity. As farmers produced more, food prices fell.	**High Costs.** Farmers had to ship their crops to market. Railroads used the lack of competition on local routes to charge higher rates for short distances.	**Indebtedness.** Farmers were constantly in debt, borrowing to make improvements, buy machinery, or to get by during a poor harvest.

THE GRANGE MOVEMENT

In 1867, the **Grange Movement** was organized by farmers. Most Grangers blamed the railroads for their difficulties. In several Midwestern states, they elected candidates to state legislatures who promised to regulate the railroads. These states passed laws regulating railroad and grain storage rates. Railroad companies challenged the new Granger laws. In **Munn v. Illinois** (1877), the Supreme Court supported state government attempts to regulate railroads. The Court reversed itself in **Wabash v. Illinois** (1886), ending state regulation of railroads. The Grangers then turned to Congress. In 1887, Congress passed the **Interstate Commerce Act**, which prohibited railroads from charging different rates to customers shipping goods an equal distance, and other unfair practices. An **Interstate Commerce Commission** was created to investigate complaints and to enforce the act.

THE POPULIST PARTY, 1891-1896

In 1892, farmers gave their support to the new **Populist Party**, which represented laborers, farmers and industrial workers in their battle against banking and railroad interests. Populists believed rich industrialists and bankers had a stranglehold on government. In 1892, the Populists held a national convention to choose a Presidential candidate. Their party platform had several innovative proposals:

Cartoon showing the many factions in the Populist Party

THE POPULIST PLATFORM (1892)

- **Unlimited Coinage of Silver** to raise farm prices and make loan repayments easier.
- **Direct Election of Senators** instead of by state legislatures.
- **Term Limits for President** permitting only a single term in office.
- **Graduated Income Tax**, taxing wealthy individuals at a higher rate.
- **Immigration Quotas** to restrict the influx of newcomers.
- **Shorter Work Day** of eight hours.

THE ELECTION OF 1896 AND THE POPULIST PARTY

In 1896, the Democratic Party nominated **William Jennings Bryan** for President after he delivered a speech at the Democratic Convention. His **"Cross of Gold"** speech denounced bankers for "crucifying mankind on a cross of gold." Although the Populists supported Bryan for President, he lost the election to Republican **William McKinley**. Bryan lost to McKinley a second time in 1900. Many Populist reforms, such as the graduated income tax and the direct election of Senators, were later passed by other political parties. The Populists illustrate a role often played by **third parties** in American politics. Third parties often provide an outlet for minority groups to voice grievances and generate new ideas.

THE PROGRESSIVE MOVEMENT, 1900-1920

The **Progressive Movement** flourished between 1900 and the start of World War I. Progressives were mainly middle-class city dwellers, rather than farmers and workers. Their activities reflected the rising influence of the middle class.

THE PROGRESSIVE MOVEMENT EMERGES

The rise of industry had brought many new social problems — brutal working conditions, child labor, political corruption, urban overcrowding, and the abuse of consumers through monopoly power. The goal of the Progressives was to correct the political and economic injustices that had resulted from America's industrialization. They sought to use the power of government to correct the evils of industrialization so that all Americans could enjoy better lives. To achieve this, the Progressives felt they also had to reform government, which they believed had been corrupted by big business and political "bosses."

THE MUCKRAKERS

Among the most influential Progressives were investigative reporters, writers, and social scientists who exposed government corruption and the abuses of industry. These writers became known as **muckrakers**. They examined the rise of industry and the abuses that often led to the accumulation of large fortunes. They also examined business practices affecting consumers and the lives of the poor.

FAMOUS MUCKRAKERS

Muckraker	Work
Jacob Riis	Photographed and described the appalling conditions of the urban poor in his book *How The Other Half Lives*.
Ida Tarbell	Her book *History of the Standard Oil Company* (1902) showed how John D. Rockefeller's rise was based on ruthless business practices.
Lincoln Steffens	Exposed corruption in city and state governments in his book *The Shame of the Cities* (1904).
Upton Sinclair	His novel *The Jungle* (1906) described the unsanitary practices of the meat-packing industry.

THE SOCIAL REFORMERS

Some Progressives were so stirred by the abuses of industrial society that they made individual efforts at reform. Settlement houses were started in slum neighborhoods by Progressives like **Jane Addams** and **Lillian Wald**. These houses provided such services as child care, nursing the sick, and teaching English to immigrants. Other Progressive groups formed associations to promote social change, such as the **N.A.A.C.P.**

Corbiss-Bettman Archives

Jane Addams

THE REFORM OF STATE AND LOCAL GOVERNMENT

Other Progressives focused on correcting abuses found at the municipal and state levels of government. Progressives replaced "boss rule" with public-minded mayors. They expanded services to deal with overcrowding, fire hazards, and the lack of public services. In some cities, Progressives introduced new forms of city government to halt corruption. Progressives governors, such as **Robert LaFollette** in Wisconsin and **Theodore Roosevelt** in New York, took steps to free their state governments from the corrupting influence of big business. Many of the measures introduced by the Progressives to state governments were later adopted at the federal level.

PROGRESSIVE POLITICAL REFORMS

Secret Ballot. Voters were less subject to pressure and intimidation when they could cast their ballots without anyone knowing who they voted for.	**Greater Participation.** Voters could introduce bills in some state legislatures. In some states, elected officials could be removed by voters in a special election.	**Direct Party Primaries.** Special elections were held among each party's members to select candidates to nominate for election.	**Direct Election of Senators.** Senators were elected directly by voters, instead of being chosen by state legislatures (the **Seventeenth Amendment**).

THE PROGRESSIVE PRESIDENTS

Between 1901 and 1919, two strong-willed Presidents, Theodore Roosevelt and Woodrow Wilson, launched a series of Progressive reforms from the White House.

THEODORE ROOSEVELT, 1901-1909

Roosevelt believed the President should exercise vigorous leadership in the public interest. In his view, the President acted as the "steward" of the people's interests.

❖ **Roosevelt as Trust-Buster.** Roosevelt revived the use of the Sherman Anti-Trust Act. He launched the break-up of Rockefeller's Standard Oil Company. Roosevelt distinguished "good trusts" from "bad trusts," rather than condemn all trusts.

❖ **Roosevelt's "Square Deal."** Roosevelt proposed new laws to protect consumer health, to regulate some industries, and to conserve the nation's natural resources. The **Meat Inspection Act** (1906) provided government inspection of meat. The **Pure Food and Drug Act** (1906) regulated food preparation and sales of medicines. Roosevelt also drew national attention to the need to conserve forests and wildlife.

WOODROW WILSON AND THE NEW FREEDOM, 1913-1921

Wilson, a Progressive Democrat, was elected President in 1912 on his promise of a **"New Freedom"** for Americans — taming big business, allowing greater competition, and eliminating special privileges. Wilson believed high tariffs benefited the rich, so he enacted a law lowering them. To make up for the lost revenues, he introduced an income tax. The Constitution had not permitted Congress to tax individuals on their income; the **Sixteenth Amendment**, ratified in 1913, gave Congress the power to do so.

The **Federal Reserve Act** (1913) reformed the banking industry by establishing Federal Reserve Banks. The act allowed the Federal Reserve Board to regulate the amount of money in circulation by controlling the amount that banks could lend. In 1914, Congress passed the **Clayton Antitrust Act**, increasing the federal government's powers to prohibit unfair business practices.

THE WOMEN'S RIGHTS MOVEMENT, 1865-1920

The Progressive Movement was accompanied by significant gains in women's rights, for which women had been fighting for nearly a century.

THE SUFFRAGE MOVEMENT

Since the founding of the United States, men had held a monopoly on authority. Women could not vote, serve on juries, or hold public office. By the mid-1800s, some women began to challenge this. In 1848, **Elizabeth Cady Stanton** and **Lucretia Mott** organized the **Seneca Falls Convention** in upstate New York. The convention passed a resolution — modeled on the Declaration of Independence — proclaiming that women were equal to men. The movement focused on **suffrage** (*the right to vote*). The lack of voting rights was seen as a symbol of women's inferior status and a as violation of basic democratic principles. **Susan B. Anthony** and other reformers won suffrage in several Western states, but were unsuccessful in introducing an amendment requiring the vote in all states.

THE TRADITIONAL ROLE OF WOMEN CHANGES, 1870-1914

Industrialization brought important changes to the traditional role of women. Free public schools opened to both boys and girls. A few colleges opened for women. Inventions such as the sewing machine, typewriter and telephone added new job opportunities for women. New labor-saving devices, such as the washing machine and vacuum cleaner, reduced housework and provided women with more leisure time.

WORLD WAR I AND THE 19TH AMENDMENT

When American men went off to fight in World War I in 1917, millions of women took their places in factories and workshops. Women's contribution to the war was the final argument in favor of women's suffrage. An amendment was introduced in Congress during the war, establishing that no state could deny a citizen the right to vote on the basis of gender. This was ratified as the **Nineteenth Amendment** in 1920.

AMERICAN FOREIGN POLICY, 1898-1920

Many Americans believed that the United States, as one of the world's leading industrial nations, should play a greater role on the world stage.

THE SPANISH-AMERICAN WAR, 1898

The Spanish-American War marked a major turning point in American foreign relations. In 1895, Cuban sugar workers rebelled against Spain, seeking their independence. A Spanish army was sent to Cuba to crush the rebellion with brutal force. Several factors led to American intervention in the conflict:

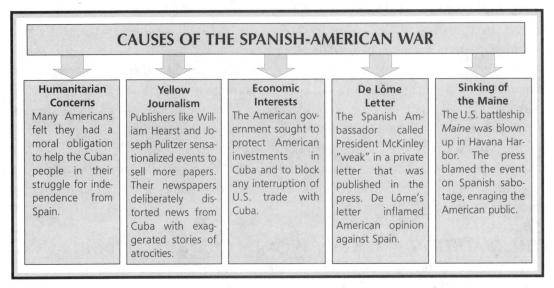

CAUSES OF THE SPANISH-AMERICAN WAR

Humanitarian Concerns	Yellow Journalism	Economic Interests	De Lôme Letter	Sinking of the Maine
Many Americans felt they had a moral obligation to help the Cuban people in their struggle for independence from Spain.	Publishers like William Hearst and Joseph Pulitzer sensationalized events to sell more papers. Their newspapers deliberately distorted news from Cuba with exaggerated stories of atrocities.	The American government sought to protect American investments in Cuba and to block any interruption of U.S. trade with Cuba.	The Spanish Ambassador called President McKinley "weak" in a private letter that was published in the press. De Lôme's letter inflamed American opinion against Spain.	The U.S. battleship *Maine* was blown up in Havana Harbor. The press blamed the event on Spanish sabotage, enraging the American public.

Shortly after the destruction of the *Maine*, President McKinley, finding it hard to resist the public outcry, asked Congress for a declaration of war against Spain. American forces quickly overcame the Spanish navy in the Philippines and Spanish troops in Cuba. As a result of the war, the United States acquired the Philippines, Puerto Rico, and Guam. Cuba became independent in name, but fell under the indirect control of the United States. The U.S. emerged from the war in possession of an overseas empire.

Library of Congress

The Maine *sinking in Havana Harbor*

AMERICA BUILDS A COLONIAL EMPIRE

Imperialism is the domination of one country by another. Opponents of U.S. imperialism felt it violated the America's democratic principles. However, many American leaders felt the moment was right for imperialism for several reasons. The United States was now an industrial power. Colonies could provide needed raw materials for factories, a guaranteed market for manufacturers, and a place for farmers to sell surplus crops. Some saw colonial expansion as a way of showing that the United States was a great nation, arguing the country should grab some colonies before nothing was left.

AMERICAN INVOLVEMENT IN THE PACIFIC AND ASIA

From the mid-1800s to the early 1900s, the U.S. acquired a colonial empire in the Pacific consisting of the Philippine Islands, Guam, Hawaii, Samoa, and Midway.

❖ **The Philippines.** Filipino rebels fought against their American colonial rulers until they were finally defeated in 1902. Philippine independence was later granted by the United States in 1946, after World War II.

Filipino rebels, 1900

❖ **Hawaii.** In the mid-19th century, American settlers built sugar and pineapple plantations on Hawaii. In the 1890s, **Queen Liliuokalani** tried to take political power away from American landowners. In response, American landowners overthrew her in 1893. After the outbreak of the Spanish-American War, Congress voted for the annexation of Hawaii in 1898. It later became the 50th state in 1959.

These new Pacific bases placed Americans in an advantageous position for trade with East Asia.

❖ **China.** The United States announced the "**Open Door Policy**," favoring equal trading rights for all foreign nations in China. In 1900, the **Boxer Rebellion** threatened foreigners in China. An international army, with U.S. participation, crushed the rebellion, but Americans opposed any attempt by other nations to use the rebellion as an excuse to dismember China.

A Chinese "Boxer"

❖ **Japan.** In 1853, the United States forced open an isolationist Japan to Western trade and influence when **Commodore Matthew Perry** landed there with American gunships. In 1905, Japan surprised the West by defeating Russia in the Russo-Japanese War. President Theodore Roosevelt brought both sides to a peace settlement in the Treaty of Portsmouth (1905).

Library of Congress

Commodore Perry lands in Japan

U.S. IMPERIALISM IN THE CARIBBEAN

The Spanish-American War also gave the U.S. direct control of Puerto Rico and indirect control of Cuba, leading to increased American interest in the Caribbean region.

❖ **Cuba.** Cubans were forced to agree to the **Platt Amendment**, which gave the United States the right to intervene in Cuban affairs at any time.

❖ **Panama Canal.** The Spanish-American War highlighted the need for a canal so the U.S. Navy could send ships between the Atlantic and Pacific Oceans without circling South America. When Panamanian rebels declared their independence from Colombia, President Theodore Roosevelt sent American warships to protect them. In return, the new government of Panama gave the U. S. control of the **Panama Canal Zone,** a 10-mile-wide strip through the center of Panama, where Americans started to built the canal in 1903. The massive project was completed in 1914, at a cost of $400 million.

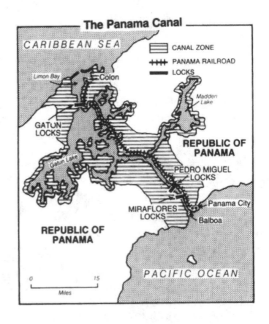

The Panama Canal

AMERICAN INTERVENTION IN LATIN AMERICA

In the late 19th and early 20th centuries, the U.S. government extended the Monroe Doctrine. In 1904, President Roosevelt declared that the U.S. would act as an "international police power" in Latin America. The so-called "Roosevelt Corollary to the Monroe Doctrine" also became known as the **Big Stick Policy**. It was used to justify sending troops to Haiti, Nicaragua, Honduras and the Dominican Republic. President Wilson intervened in both the Caribbean region and Mexico. Wilson finally withdrew U.S. troops from Mexico in 1917, when America faced involvement in World War I.

THE UNITED STATES IN WORLD WAR I

Since the War of 1812, American leaders had successfully avoided "entanglements" with Europe. Another turning point in U.S. foreign policy was reached when America entered World War I in 1917.

REASONS FOR U.S. INTERVENTION

War broke out in Europe in 1914 when Austria tried to avenge the assassination of Archduke Francis Ferdinand by attacking Serbia. Other leading powers were pulled into the conflict by their alliance commitments. Germany aided Austria, while Britain, France and Russia joined on the Serbian side. Woodrow Wilson, who had successfully campaigned for the Presidency on a promise to keep the U.S. out of war, attempted to follow the traditional American policy of neutrality. Despite his efforts, the United States eventually became involved in the conflict.

❖ **German Actions and Allied Propaganda.** Americans were shocked at the German invasion of neutral Belgium. The **Zimmerman Telegram**, a secret message from a high German official promised to return territories to Mexico if Mexico helped Germany against the United States. American public opinion was outraged when the telegram was printed in the newspapers.

❖ **Violation of Freedom of the Seas.** The main reason for American entry into World War I was unrestricted German submarine warfare. In 1915, a German submarine sank the British passenger ship *Lusitania*, killing over 1,000 passengers, including 128 Americans. Wilson threatened to break off relations with Germany. Germany pledged not to sink any ocean liners without prior warning. However, German submarines began to attack American merchant vessels again in 1917. In response, Wilson asked Congress to declare war.

AMERICA AT WAR, 1917-1918

To fight the war, Wilson was given sweeping powers. He established several agencies to regulate the economy. Congress passed the **Selective Service Act** (1917) to draft men for the army.

During the war, civil liberties were curtailed. In *Schenck v. U.S.* (1919), the Supreme Court upheld restrictions on free speech if such speech caused "a clear and present danger" to the nation.

An American soldier bids his sweeetheart goodbye before leaving for Europe

THE PEACE SETTLEMENT

American troops broke the deadlock in Europe, causing Germany to enter into an armistice *(an agreement to stop fighting)* in 1918. Wilson had already announced America's war aims in the **Fourteen Points** — they called for freedom of the seas, reduced armaments, and an end to secret diplomacy. Wilson felt the most important part of his plan was a **League of Nations** that would discourage future wars. Wilson traveled to Europe to help negotiate the peace treaties. The final terms of the **Treaty of Versailles** and the other peace treaties were extremely harsh on Germany and the other defeated powers, but the treaties did at least establish the League of Nations that Wilson had proposed.

AMERICA RETREATS INTO ISOLATIONISM

Wilson's opponents believed the League might drag Americans into unnecessary warfare overseas. Although Wilson needed the Senate to ratify the Versailles Treaty, he rejected any compromises proposed by the Senators. Wilson failed to gauge the feelings of most Americans, who were disillusioned with involvement in world affairs. The Senate rejected the treaty, and the United States never joined the League. This move marked a return to a policy of **isolationism** — refusing to become involved in other countries' conflicts.

Wilson (r.) with other Allied leaders at the Versailles peace conference

SUMMARIZING YOUR UNDERSTANDING

KEY TERMS, CONCEPTS, AND PEOPLE

- ✦ Grange Movement
- ✦ Populist Party
- ✦ Progressive Movement

- ✦ Muckrakers
- ✦ Theodore Roosevelt
- ✦ Woodrow Wilson

- ✦ Imperialism
- ✦ Fourteen Points
- ✦ League of Nations

MULTIPLE-CHOICE QUESTIONS

1 A major aim of both the Grange and Populist Movements was
   1 the establishment of a gold standard for currency
   2 mandatory government policies to curb inflation
   3 the passage of laws to regulate monopolies
   4 unlimited immigration by Asians

2 The Granger Laws were an attempt by various state legislatures to regulate
   1 farmers   3 manufacturers
   2 railroads   4 factories

3 Which contributed most to the birth of the Progressive Movement?
   1 the influence of muckrakers, Populists, and social reformers
   2 the start of World War I
   3 racial conflict in the New South
   4 the migration of population from cities to the countryside

4 The muckrakers of the Progressive Era and the investigative reporters of today are
   most similar in that both
   1 sought to document corruption in American life
   2 advocated fewer government controls on the economy
   3 tried to increase the spirit of patriotism
   4 called for increased aid to economically less developed nations

5 A study of the Progressive Movement would indicate the Progressives sought to
   1 ease immigration requirements   3 defeat the Populist platform
   2 correct abuses of industrial society 4 support big business

6 President Theodore Roosevelt was referred to as a "trustbuster" because he
   1 introduced new foreign policies   3 enacted a business tax
   2 supported big business   4 attacked business monopolies

7 The Women's Rights Movement of the late 19th century primarily focused its efforts on securing
  1 Cabinet positions for women   3 equal rights for all minorities
  2 the reform of prisons   4 suffrage for women

8 The major purpose of the Federal Reserve Act (1913) was to
  1 allow a flexible money supply   3 insure people's bank deposits
  2 compete with state banks   4 implement a graduated income tax

9 In *Schenck v. United States*, the Supreme Court decided that a "clear and present danger" to the United States permitted
  1 an expansion of Presidential power   3 creation of a peacetime draft
  2 restrictions on 1st Amendment rights   4 limitations on the right to vote

10 A principal reason why isolationists in the U.S. Senate objected to joining the League of Nations was their opposition to
  1 lower tariffs   3 potential military commitments
  2 freedom of the seas   4 reparation payments by Germany

THEMATIC ESSAY QUESTION

Directions: Write a well-organized essay that includes an introduction, several paragraphs addressing the task, and a conclusion.

Theme: Presidential Actions

> Throughout our history, specific actions taken by U.S. Presidents have either increased or decreased the role of the federal government in American life.

Task:

> From your study of United States history, identify **two** U.S. Presidents.
> For *each* President identified:
> - *Discuss* one specific action taken by that President that had an impact on the role of the federal government in American life.
> - *Explain how* this action either increased or decreased the role of the federal government at that time.

You may use actions taken by any President from your study of U. S. history. Some suggestions you might consider include: George Washington, Thomas Jefferson, Andrew Jackson, Abraham Lincoln, Theodore Roosevelt, and Woodrow Wilson.
You are *not* limited to these suggestions.

DOCUMENT-BASED QUESTION

This question is based on the accompanying documents (1-7). This question is designed to test your ability to work with historical documents. Some of the documents have been edited for the purposes of the question. As you analyze the documents, take into account both the source of each document and any point of view that may be presented in the document.

Historical Context: The decision to go to war is among the gravest choices made by any nation. Throughout history, Americans have made this choice for a variety of reasons.

Task: Using information from the documents and your knowledge of U.S. history, answer the questions that follow each document in Part A. Your answers to the questions will help you write the Part B essay, in which you will be asked to:

> Compare and contrast the various reasons why
> Americans have become involved in wars.

Part A — Short Answer Questions

Directions: Analyze each document and answer the questions that follow it.

Document 1:

> *Whenever any form of government becomes destructive* [of the people's rights] *it is the right of the people to alter or abolish it.... The history of the present King of Great Britain is the history of repeated injuries .... all having in direct object the establishment of an absolute tyranny over these states. He has obstructed the administration of justice. He has kept among us .... standing armies, without the consent of our legislatures."*
> — Declaration of Independence, July 4, 1776

1. According to the Declaration, why were Americans justified in fighting Britain?

_____

Document 2:

> "My [main] *object in this struggle is to save the Union, and is not either to save or destroy slavery. If I could save the Union without freeing any slave, I would do it; if I could save it by freeng all the slaves, I would do it; and if I could do it by freeing some and leaving others alone, I would also do that."*
> — Abraham Lincoln's reply to the *New York Tribune*, August 22, 1862

2. What did Lincoln argue was his main reason for involvement in the Civil War?

_____

Document 3:

> "*Slavery was of less importance to the seceding States than the recognition of the federal principle. The conflict was a conflict between those who were for maintaining the federal character of the government, and those who were for centralizing all power in the federal head. It was a conflict between the supporters of the Union established by the Constitution, and those who wanted to overthrow this union of states and to erect a national consolidation in its place.*"
>
> — Alexander H. Stephens, former Confederate Vice-President

3. What did Stephens see as the main cause of the conflict between the states?

_____

Document 4:

> "*The horrors of the barbarous struggle for the extermination of the native population are witnessed in all parts of the country. Blood on the roadsides, blood in the fields, blood on the door-steps, blood, blood, blood! The old, the young, the weak, the crippled, all are butchered without mercy.*"
>
> — Article in Joseph Pulitzer's *New York World* describing Spanish atrocities in Cuba, 1896

4. How did articles like these contribute to the outbreak of the Spanish-American War? _____

Document 5:

5. What is the main idea of this political cartoon?

_____

_____

_____

_____

_____

"The Spanish Brute"

Document 6:

6. How did the policy announced in this proclamation eventually bring the United States into World War I? _____

_____

_____

_____

_____

_____

ADMIRALTY PROCLAMATION

The waters surrounding Great Britain and Iceland, including the English channel, are hereby declared to be within the war zone, and all enemy merchant vessels found in those waters after the eighteen of February, 1915 will be destroyed. In addition, it may not always be possible to save crews and passengers...

Danger to neutral vessels within this zone of war cannot always be avoided and neutral vessels may suffer from attacks intended to strike enemy ships.

— **German Admiralty**

Document 7:

THE NEW YORK TIMES

Vol. LXIV	New York, Saturday, May 8, 1915	One Cent

LUSITANIA SUNK BY GERMAN SUBMARINE
TWICE TORPEDOED OFF IRISH COAST
PROBABLY 1,260 DEAD, 128 ARE AMERICANS
WASHINGTON SEES A CRISIS AT HAND

7A. Why would a German submarine attack the British passenger ship *Lusitania*?

_____

7B. How did this newspaper headline serve to inflame American public opinion?

_____

_____

Document 8

> *"We intend to begin unrestricted submarine warfare in February [1916]. We [seek] to keep the United States neutral. In the event of our not succeeding, we [offer to] Mexico a proposal: Make war together, make peace together, generous financial support, and an understanding that Mexico [will be given] the lost territories of Texas, New Mexico, and Arizona. Inform the President of Mexico of the above as soon as the outbreak of war with the United States...."*
>
> — Telegram by the Minister Zimmerman to the German Ambassador in Mexico

8a. What did Germany promise to Mexico in this proposal? _____
_____

8b. Why was American public opinion inflamed against Germany after this telegram was made public? _____

Part B — Essay

Directions:
Using information from the documents provided, and your knowledge of United States history, write a well-organized essay that includes an introduction, several paragraphs, and a conclusion.

Historical Context:
The decision to go to war is among the gravest choices made by any nation. Throughout history, Americans have made this choice for a variety of reasons.

Task: Using information from the documents and your knowledge of United States history, write an essay in which you:

> * *Compare and contrast* various reasons why Americans have gone to war.
> * *Evaluate* the effects of **one** of the wars related to these documents.

Guidelines: Be sure to
* Address all aspects of the *Task* by accurately analyzing and interpreting at least **four** documents
* Incorporate information from the documents in the body of the essay
* Incorporate relevant outside information throughout the essay
* Richly support the theme with relevant facts, examples, and details
* Write a well-developed essay that consistently demonstrates a logical and clear play of organization
* Introduce the theme by establishing a framework that is beyond a simple restatement of the *Task* or *Historical Context,* and conclude the essay with a summation of the theme.

CHAPTER 8

PROSPERITY AND DEPRESSION

In this chapter, you will learn how the nation entered a new age of prosperity in the 1920s. Automobiles, telephones and electricity made life more convenient and comfortable than ever before. Unfortunately, this prosperity was cut short by the Great Depression. This depression turned out to be the worst economic crisis in American history. President Herbert Hoover's measures proved unable to restore economic growth. Under his successor, Franklin D. Roosevelt, the federal government intervened on a massive scale to restore employment. In this chapter you will learn about the following:

Library of Congress

A photograph taken by Dorothea Lange during the Great Depression

- **The Roaring Twenties.** In the 1920s, the automobile and other new technologies contributed to growing prosperity, as did Republican policies that were favorable to business. Mass consumption led to new cultural values, such as new roles for women. Farmers and minorities failed to share in the decade's benefits.

- **The Great Depression.** Overproduction, speculation, and the lack of buying power among many groups set the stage for the Great Depression. When the New York Stock Market crashed in 1929, banks failed, markets declined, and businesses went bankrupt. Soon millions of people were out of work.

- **The New Deal.** President Franklin D. Roosevelt introduced policies of relief, recovery, and reform to revive the economy, including the Social Security Act and the Wagner Act. The New Deal greatly increased the size, power and responsibilities of the federal government.

In studying this period, you should focus on the following questions:
- ✦ What factors contributed to the economic prosperity of the Roaring '20s?
- ✦ What were the causes of the Great Depression?
- ✦ What has been the impact of the New Deal?

BOOM TIMES: THE 1920s

THE ROARING TWENTIES, 1919-1929

The "**Roaring Twenties**" were good times for many Americans. But beneath an appearance of calm and prosperity, America was experiencing fundamental economic and social changes.

ADJUSTING TO PEACE, 1919-1920

At first, the nation faced the difficult task of adjusting to peace — the government stopped its wartime spending and soldiers returned home looking for jobs, creating a recession from 1919 to 1921. There were also attacks on civil liberties. When a wave of strikes hit the nation in 1919, citizens feared they were seeing the beginning of a Communist revolution. This "**Red Scare**" led **Attorney General Palmer** to arrest radicals accused of plotting to overthrow the government. Soon afterwards, two immigrants, **Sacco and Vanzetti**, were convicted of murder to get funds for an anarchist revolution. Although the evidence was insufficient, they were found guilty and executed.

RISE OF NATIVISM

The "Red Scare" and the Sacco and Vanzetti trial greatly contributed to the rise of **nativism** — a dislike of foreigners. The **Immigration Acts** of 1921, 1924, and 1929 restricted immigration from Southern and Eastern Europe (the "New Immigrants") by establishing quotas for each nationality based on America's existing ethnic composition.

THE REPUBLICAN PRESIDENCIES

In 1920, Republicans returned to the White House. In general, Presidents Harding, Coolidge and Hoover supported laissez-faire economic policies, with minimal interference in business activities.

❖ **The Harding Administration** (1921-1923). Warren Harding captured the national spirit by calling for a "return to normalcy." However, the **Teapot Dome Scandal** revealed that a high-ranking administration official had been bribed to lease oil-rich government lands at Teapot Dome, Wyoming, to businessmen.

❖ **The Coolidge Administration** (1923-1929). Calvin Coolidge symbolized old-fashioned values like honesty and thrift. Continuing Harding's policies, Coolidge's motto embodied his philosophy: "The business of America is business."

❖ **The Hoover Administration** (1929-1933). In his 1928 campaign for President, Herbert Hoover predicted an end to poverty in America. He believed America's achievement in raising living standards was the result of a system in which individuals were given equal opportunities, a free education, and a will to succeed. This "**rugged individualism**," as Hoover called it, spurred progress. He strongly felt that government interference in business could threaten the nation's prosperity.

FACTORS UNDERLYING PROSPERITY

For many Americans, the 1920s were prosperous times. Wages and employment opportunities increased, while business profits and production soared. Government policies favoring business were one factor. Others factors included:

THE RISE OF THE AUTOMOBILE AND OTHER INDUSTRIES

The growth in automobile ownership greatly affected American life. Automobile production required vast amounts of steel, glass, and rubber — stimulating those industries. Cars gave people much greater mobility. The growth of suburbs was made possible by the car. School buses allowed students in remote areas to attend school regularly for the first time. Farmers replaced draft animals with tractors. Besides automobiles, other new industries developed, largely based on new uses of electricity. Household appliances, like the vacuum cleaner, refrigerator and toaster, were

Ford Motor Company

Henry Ford poses next to the ten-millionth Model T

introduced. Radio and motion pictures became widespread. These industries created new jobs, and changed the ways Americans lived.

MORE EFFICIENT PRODUCTION TECHNIQUES

Henry Ford introduced the **assembly line** to automobile production in 1914. The assembly line, the use of standardized parts, and other labor-saving devices made American industry more efficient and productive, while lowering costs.

THE AGE OF MASS CONSUMPTION

The 1920s witnessed new patterns of consumption, creating mass markets for goods. Advertising stimulated demand, while workers with higher wages and more leisure time had greater purchasing power. Retailers developed programs for installment purchases and buying on credit.

SPECULATION BOOM

The development growth of new industries, improved production techniques and mass markets helped fuel a speculative boom on the New York Stock Exchange, where millions of people invested in the hope of striking it rich.

CULTURAL VALUES OF THE 1920s

The 1920s also saw the emergence of new values. Many groups, especially women, African Americans and young people felt a new sense of power and freedom. Others felt threatened and sought to preserve traditional values.

ATTEMPTS TO PRESERVE TRADITIONAL VALUES

At the start of the 1920s, rural America continued to regard the rise of urban society with suspicion.

A government offical smashes a barrel of beer during Prohibition

❖ **Prohibition**. Reformers often saw liquor as the cause of poverty and crime. In 1919, the **Eighteenth Amendment** was ratified, banning the sale of all alcoholic drinks. Gradually Americans began to see this "experiment" as a failure, since many people refused to accept the ban on alcohol. In addition, the great demand for illegal liquor stimulated the growth of organized crime in the 1920s. Prohibition was repealed in 1933 by the **Twenty-first Amendment**. Americans learned from this experience that widely unpopular laws are sometimes unenforceable.

❖ **The Scopes "Monkey" Trial**. Tennessee passed a law that forbade teaching Darwin's theory of evolution because it contradicted the Bible's account of Creation. In 1925, John Scopes, a biology teacher, was tried and convicted for teaching evolution. The trial helped to illustrate the clash between new scientific theories and some older religious beliefs.

THE EMERGENCE OF NEW VALUES

In opposition to traditional values were the newer values of the period, which encouraged greater openness and self-expression.

❖ **Women**. New appliances reduced housework, and more women went to college. As more women worked, they demonstrated a new economic independence and became more assertive. Women began to smoke and drink in public. Younger women rejected restrictive clothing in favor of shorter hair and skirts above the knees, went out on dates unchaperoned, and danced the Charleston.

Women working at the U.S. Treasury

❖ **Youth and the Lost Generation**. A new group of writers, known as the Lost Generation, rejected the desire for material wealth. Novelists such as **Sinclair Lewis**, in *Main Street* and *Babbitt*, ridiculed the narrowness and hypocrisy of American life. In *The Great Gatsby*, **F. Scott Fitzgerald** hinted that the search for purely material success often led to tragedy.

❖ **The Harlem Renaissance**. The 1920s is often referred to as the **Jazz Age**, reflecting the greater importance of African-American music. The migration of African Americans to Northern cities increased in the 1920s. The center of African-American life at that time was Harlem, where jazz flourished. An awakening of African-American culture in these years became known as the "Harlem Renaissance." African-American writers such as **Langston Hughes** and **Countee Cullen** expressed a new pride in their heritage, while attacking racism.

THE GREAT DEPRESSION, 1929-1940

Economies historically pass through good and bad periods that usually repeat themselves. The bad times are called **depressions** — characterized by business failures and high unemployment. The **Great Depression** was the worst in our nation's history.

CAUSES OF THE GREAT DEPRESSION

A variety of factors caused the economy to move from the prosperity of the 1920s to the severe depression of the 1930s.

OVERPRODUCTION

The 1920s saw the rapid introduction of many new products like cars, radios and refrigerators. Companies were soon producing more goods than people could afford to buy.

UNEVEN DISTRIBUTION OF INCOME

Even in the 1920s, not all groups shared in the national prosperity. Many African Americans, Hispanics, Native American Indians, farmers and industrial workers still faced hard times.

SPECULATION

In the 1920s, stocks soared in value. Many people bought stocks hoping to "get rich quick." This drove stock prices even higher. To make matters worse, people were buying stocks on margin — paying only a small percentage of a stock's value while promising to pay the rest later, when they sold the stock. People invested in real estate with similar hopes of getting rich quickly. The frenzy of stock market and real estate speculation created an atmosphere of easy money.

SHAKY BANKING

The government failed to regulate effectively either the banking system or the stock market. Bankers often invested their depositors' money in unsound investments. Many consumers were buying more than they could afford, on credit. This vast overextension of debt made the entire economy vulnerable.

THE GREAT DEPRESSION BEGINS

When the New York Stock Market crashed in 1929, it set off a chain reaction that toppled the American economy and quickly spread to the rest of the world.

THE STOCK MARKET CRASH

On October 29, 1929, prices on the New York Stock Exchange began to plunge, and soon hit all-time lows. Corporations could no longer raise funds. People were unable to repay their loans or rents, leading to bank failures. Thousands of people lost their life savings. In this new economic climate, the demand for goods decreased sharply. As prices fell, factories closed and workers lost their jobs. Demand was reduced still further, causing prices to fall more. Other factories closed, and the country became caught in the grip of a vicious downward spiral.

THE HUMAN IMPACT OF THE GREAT DEPRESSION

Businesses closed, farmers lost their farms, banks failed, and millions of people were out of work. Unlike today, there was no "safety net" — unemployment insurance and bank deposit insurance did not exist. Private charities were overwhelmed. People lost their homes and went hungry. Millions depended on soup kitchens for food.

THE DUST BOWL

In addition to the financial disaster, the farmers of the Great Plains faced natural disasters in the 1930s. Since the 1870s, farmers had been tilling the Great Plains, cutting the grasses that had covered the topsoil, and tapping underground water supplies. A series of droughts in the early 1930s dried up crops and topsoil, turning the soil into dust. Heavy

National Archives

Farm machinery buried under a sea of dust

winds destroyed harvests and carried soil away in huge clouds of dust that darkened the sky for miles. Farmers, unable to grow enough to pay their bills, often abandoned their land. Many farmers moved west to California.

PRESIDENT HOOVER FAILS TO HALT THE DEPRESSION

Despite the economic catastrophe, President Hoover rejected demands for the federal government to provide direct payments to the unemployed and needy. He believed that voluntary and private organizations should provide emergency relief. Hoover was convinced that when prices fell low enough, people would resume buying and employment would increase. Unfortunately, his predictions were incorrect. Later, Hoover did cut taxes, increased federal spending on public projects, and directed a federal agency to buy surplus farm crops. However, his policies were too little, too late. Shanty towns of the homeless and unemployed, sarcastically called "**Hoovervilles**," sprang up on the outskirts of cities.

FRANKLIN D. ROOSEVELT AND THE NEW DEAL

The Governor of New York, **Franklin D. Roosevelt,** easily defeated Hoover in the Presidential election of 1932. Roosevelt promised Americans a "**New Deal**," to put them back to work.

ROOSEVELT INTRODUCES THE NEW DEAL

The New Deal was a major turning point in American history. It established the principle that the federal government bears the chief responsibility for ensuring the smooth running of the American economy.

ROOSEVELT'S NEW DEAL PHILOSOPHY

President Roosevelt saw that the Great Depression was a national emergency. He believed the President's task was to find a way for the economy to return to prosperity. The New Deal marked an end to the long-held view that government and the economy should be separated. The New Deal permanently increased the size and power of the federal government, making it primarily responsible for managing the nation's economy.

Franklin D Roosevelt Library

Roosevelt and his "Brain Trust" — a group of talented people who helped him deal with the problems of the nation

NEW DEAL LEGISLATION; RELIEF, RECOVERY, REFORM

As soon as President Roosevelt took office, he called Congress into special session. Roosevelt pushed through legislation in his first 100 days in office that would have been difficult to pass in less critical times. Roosevelt explained the New Deal measures in terms of three R's — **Relief, Recovery,** and **Reform.**

❖ **Relief** measures were short-term actions to tide people over until the economy recovered. Over one-quarter of the nation's workforce was unemployed. There was no unemployment insurance. Many people who were out of work had no food or shelter. Roosevelt favored giving people emergency public jobs.

- **Civilian Conservation Corps** (1933) gave jobs to young people, such as planting trees and cleaning up forests. Members of the C.C.C. lived in camps and received free food. Most of their pay was sent to their parents.

- **Works Progress Administration** (1935). The W.P.A. created jobs by hiring artists, writers and musicians to paint murals, write plays and compose music.

❖ **Recovery** measures were designed to restore the economy by increasing incentives to produce and by rebuilding people's purchasing power.

- **National Recovery Administration** (1933) asked businesses to voluntarily follow codes which set prices, production limits and a minimum wage. However, in 1935, the Supreme Court found the N.R.A. unconstitutional.

- **Agricultural Adjustment Acts.** In the first A.A.A., the government paid farmers to plant less in the hope of increasing crop prices. In 1936, the Supreme Court declared the A.A.A. unconstitutional. In 1938, the second A.A.A. succeeded in raising farm prices by having the government buy farm surpluses and storing them until prices went up.

❖ **Reform** measures were aimed at remedying defects in the structure of the nation's economy, to ensure another depression would never strike again.

"REFORM" LEGISLATION DURING THE NEW DEAL

LEGISLATION	DESCRIPTION
Federal Deposit Insurance Corporation (1933)	Insured bank deposits so that people would not lose their savings in case a bank failed.
Securities and Exchange Commission (1934)	Created to oversee the operations of the stock market, prevent fraud and guard against another stock market collapse.
National Labor Relations Act (1935)	Often called the **Wagner Act**, it gave workers the right to form unions to bargain collectively with their employer.
Social Security Act (1935)	Provided workers with unemployment insurance, old age pensions, and insurance if they died early.

REACTIONS TO THE NEW DEAL

Roosevelt's efforts to combat the depression made him very popular, giving him a victory in the 1936 Presidential election. By the next election, in 1940, Europe was in the middle of World War II. Roosevelt broke with tradition by running for a third term, and was again re-elected. In 1944, Roosevelt successfully ran for a fourth term. Only one year later, Roosevelt died. The **Twenty-second Amendment** was ratified in 1951, limiting future Presidents to no more than two elected terms.

FRANKLIN D. ROOSEVELT'S COURT PACKING SCHEME

In 1935-36, the Court ruled the N.R.A. and A.A.A. unconstitutional. Roosevelt feared that the Court might declare other New Deal legislation unconstitutional. In 1937, he proposed adding six new justices to the Supreme Court to give him control of the Court. The plan was seen as an attempt to upset the traditional balance of power. Roosevelt's scheme was condemned by the public and later rejected by Congress. However, the Supreme Court stopped overturning New Deal legislation.

CHECKING YOUR UNDERSTANDING

KEY TERMS, CONCEPTS, AND PEOPLE

- ✦ Red Scare
- ✦ Sacco and Vanzetti Trial
- ✦ Teapot Dome Scandal
- ✦ Harlem Renaissance
- ✦ Dust Bowl
- ✦ Franklin D. Roosevelt
- ✦ New Deal
- ✦ Social Security Act
- ✦ Court-Packing Plan

MULTIPLE-CHOICE QUESTIONS

1   What might someone be called who supported immigration quotas, the execution of Sacco and Vanzetti, and the rebirth of the Ku Klux Klan?
   1 a rugged individualist
   2 an imperialist
   3 a nativist
   4 a mercantilist

2   The "Harlem Renaissance" refers to the
   1 artistic style of the first Dutch settlers in New York
   2 regiment of African-American soldiers in World War I
   3 flourishing of African-American literature and music during the 1920s
   4 blossoming of Hispanic culture in New York during the 1960s

3   Which was an immediate effect of the use of new production techniques during the period 1900 to 1929?
   1 a decline in the work ethic
   2 an increase in consumer products
   3 a decline in business profits
   4 an increased unemployment rate

4   What was an important effect of the automobile industry's growth after World War I?
   1 It stimulated the growth of several other industries.
   2 There were decreased employment opportunities.
   3 There was an increased number of railroad passengers.
   4 It encouraged government control of major industries.

5   Which lesson is best supported by a study of Prohibition?
   1 Social attitudes can make some laws difficult to enforce.
   2 Increased taxes can affect consumer spending.
   3 Morality can be legislated successfully.
   4 People will sacrifice willingly for the common good.

6   Which was an important cause of the Great Depression?
   1 speculation on the stock market
   2 shortages of consumer goods
   3 the collapse of the gold standard
   4 higher oil and farm prices

7   Which statement best describes Franklin Roosevelt's New Deal programs?
    1   They reduced the number of government employees.
    2   They expanded the role of government in the economy.
    3   They stressed the need for local government leadership.
    4   They emphasized the importance of the gold standard.

8   The primary purpose of the Social Security Act of 1935 was to
    1   achieve integrated public schools
    2   provide old age and unemployment insurance
    3   regulate international trade
    4   guarantee collective bargaining

9   Opponents of the New Deal claimed these programs violated the tradition of
    1   welfare capitalism   3   government regulation of business
    2   collective bargaining   4   individual responsibility

10 Roosevelt's election to a *fourth* Presidential term can be attributed to the
    1   blame placed on Republicans for the country's economic problems
    2   need to continue efforts to cope with rising farm prices
    3   unwillingness of voters to change leadership during a major war
    4   lack of a strong opposition candidate

THEMATIC ESSAY QUESTION

Directions: Write a well-organized essay that includes an introduction, several paragraphs addressing the task below, and a conclusion.

Theme: Economic Problems

Economic problems have been a major concern of Americans since the Civil War.

Task:

Choose **two** economic problems from your study of American history.
For *each* economic problem:
• *Describe* the economic problem.
• *Show how* that economic problem was dealt with by the federal government.

You may use any examples from your study of United States history and government. Some suggestions you might consider include: a lack of funds in the U.S. Treasury, the rise of monopolies, the problems of farmers, unemployment, inflation, and the abuse of workers or consumers.

You are *not* limited to these suggestions.

CHAPTER 9

THE AGE OF GLOBAL CRISIS

In the 1920s and 1930s, dictatorships came to power in Italy, Germany and other countries. When war broke out in Europe and Asia, Americans were reluctant to become involved. However, Japan's attack on Pearl Harbor, Hawaii on December 7, 1941 ended U.S. neutrality. American participation helped achieve an Allied victory in World War II. U.S. leaders later regretted not having stamped out Nazi aggression in its infancy. In the post-war years, they resolved not to make the same mistake when combatting the spread of Communism in the world. In this chapter you will learn about the following:

National Archives

An atom bomb is dropped on Nagasaki, 1945

- **American Isolationism**. After World War I, America became isolationist in foreign affairs. When war began in Europe in 1939, the U.S. remained neutral.

- **The United States in World War II**. On December 7, 1941, Japanese planes bombed Pearl Harbor. This action pushed the United States into the war against Germany, Japan, and Italy. After a long struggle, the Allies achieved victory in 1945. Germany was divided, and Japan was occupied by U.S. forces.

- **The Cold War**. Immediately following World War II, the United States and the Soviet Union became rivals in the "Cold War," which quickly spread from Europe to Asia. American leaders took steps to contain Communism.

In studying this period, you should focus on the following questions:

✦ Why was the United States isolationist in the years 1920-1941?
✦ What factors led to the outbreak of World War II?
✦ What were the causes of the Cold War?
✦ How did U.S. leaders attempt to contain Communism in Europe and Asia?

AMERICAN ISOLATIONISM, 1920-1941

In the 1920s the U.S. returned to its traditional policy of **isolationism**. America refused to join the League of Nations, passed high tariffs on European goods, and restricted European immigration There were some exceptions to this trend. In 1921, **Americans hosted the Washington Naval Conference**, in which major powers agreed to limit the size of their navies. In 1928, the U. S. joined 61 nations in signing the **Kellogg-Briand Peace Pact**, renouncing the use of war as an instrument of national policy. Presidents Herbert Hoover and Franklin D. Roosevelt rejected Theodore Roosevelt's "Big Stick" policy and tried to improve relations with Latin America. Under the **"Good Neighbor Policy,"** the U. S. agreed not to interfere in the internal affairs of Latin American nations.

THE ORIGINS OF WORLD WAR II IN EUROPE
The spread of the Great Depression in the 1930s to Europe brought Adolf Hitler to power in Germany. Nazi aggression was the major cause of World War II.

THE FAILURE OF THE LEAGUE OF NATIONS
The League of Nations, with the responsibility of preventing another war, proved powerless against Nazi aggression. The idea of **collective security** — that peaceful nations would band together to stop aggressors — failed because major powers like the United States and the Soviet Union had refused to join the League of Nations.

APPEASEMENT FAILS AND WORLD WAR II BEGINS
In 1938, Hitler demanded the **Sudetenland** — a part of Czechoslovakia. At the **Munich Conference**, British and French leaders gave in to Hitler's demand in order to avoid war. This policy of giving in to the demands of a potential enemy is known as **appeasement**. Appeasement only encouraged Hitler to make further territorial demands. In 1939, Hitler made new demands in Poland. Fearing Hitler intended to dominate Europe, Britain and France refused to give in. When Germany invaded Poland in 1939, Britain and France felt they had no choice but to declare war.

AMERICA'S ATTEMPT AT NEUTRALITY FAILS
As tensions rose in Europe, Congress passed a series of acts to keep the country out of war. America had been drawn into World War I when German submarines attacked American ships. To avoid a repetition of this problem, the **Neutrality Acts** prohibited Americans from selling arms to warring nations or traveling on their ships.

AMERICA PREPARES FOR WAR

Americans hoped to avoid war but began making preparations in case they were dragged into the conflict. Congress increased spending on the army and navy. In 1940, just after Nazi Germany defeated France, Congress enacted the first peacetime draft.

❖ **The Lend-Lease Act**. Roosevelt pushed through the Lend-Lease Act to sell, lease, or lend war materials to "any country whose defense the President deems vital to the defense of the United States." Under this act, the United States gave more than $50 million to Britain. American battleships began protecting British ships crossing the Atlantic.

❖ **The Atlantic Charter**. In 1941, Roose-velt told Americans he hoped in the fu-ture to establish a world based on "**Four Freedoms:**" freedom of speech and ex-pression, freedom of religion, freedom from want, and freedom from fear. Roosevelt and Churchill signed the At-lantic Charter later that year, laying the foundation for the future United Nations.

The Atlantic Charter Conference

THE UNITED STATES ENTERS WORLD WAR II

Surprisingly, events in East Asia, rather than Europe, finally brought the United States into the war. Japanese leaders decided to attack and conquer Indonesia to obtain oil for their war effort. Realizing that such a move might bring America into the war, they decided to attack the United States first. Japanese leaders believed that Americans would quickly tire of the war and negotiate a compromise peace — leaving Japan in control of East Asia.

THE UNITED STATES AT WAR, 1941-1945

On December 7, 1941, Japanese airplanes attacked the U.S. Pacific fleet stationed in **Pearl Harbor**, Hawaii, destroying many ships and causing a large number of deaths. The next day, President Roosevelt asked Congress to declare war on Japan. Four days later, Germany and Italy, allies of Japan, declared war on the United States. Americans were now engaged in a war on two fronts — in Europe and in the Pacific.

THE HOME FRONT

The U.S. government now faced the giant task of mobilizing American manpower and production to meet its enormous wartime needs.

THE WAR EFFORT AT HOME	
The Draft	All men between 18 and 45 were liable for military service. For the first time, women could enlist. One out of every ten Americans served in the war.
The Labor Force	The draft and the expansion of production brought a final end to the Great Depression. Women, African Americans and other minorities filled the gap in available jobs, as other workers went to war.
Paying for the War	The war cost Americans $350 billion — ten times the cost of World War I. Americans bought war bonds, to be repaid with interest by the government after the war. The United States changed from a creditor to a debtor nation.

THE FORCED RELOCATION OF JAPANESE-AMERICANS

The attack on Pearl Harbor made many Americans fear that Japanese Americans might commit acts of sabotage. Roosevelt ordered Japanese Americans relocated to internment camps, where they lived in primitive conditions. Roosevelt justified this as a military necessity. The Supreme Court upheld these relocations in *Korematsu v. U.S.* (1944). More recently, the U.S. Congress apologized for these forced relocations.

THE WAR AGAINST GERMANY AND JAPAN

Roosevelt decided to focus his energies on defeating Germany first. By the time the U.S. entered the war, Hitler controlled most of Europe and North Africa.

❖ **The War in Europe.** Hitler made his greatest mistake when he invaded the Soviet Union and declared war on the United States before defeating Britain. Roosevelt and Churchill promised Stalin they would open a second front against Germany in the west. Late in 1942, Allied troops landed in North Africa. After defeating German forces there, the Allies advanced to Sicily and Italy in 1943-1944. Meanwhile, Soviet forces defeated the German army at Stalingrad and advanced westward toward Germany.

❖ **The Collapse of Nazi Germany.** On June 6, 1944 — **D-Day** — Allied troops landed in France. They quickly moved eastward, soon reaching the German border. U.S., British and Free French forces invaded Germany from the west, while Soviet forces entered Germany from the east. In April of 1945, Hitler committed suicide. The next month, the Soviets captured Berlin and Germany surrendered.

❖ **The War against Japan**. In these same years, the United States was also at war with Japan. At first, the Japanese made significant gains in Asia and the Pacific. In 1943, the tide began to turn. The United States regained naval superiority in the Pacific, and American forces began "island-hopping" — liberating Pacific islands from Japanese control, one at a time.

❖ **The Decision to Use the Atomic Bomb**. American scientists developed the atomic bomb, which was ready for use by 1945. With Germany defeated, America was preparing to invade Japan. Harry Truman, who had become President when Roosevelt died, feared an invasion might lead to a million American casualties. Truman decided to use the atomic bomb rather than risk sustaining such losses. On August 6, an atomic bomb exploded over **Hiroshima**. Three days later, **Nagasaki** was

The devastation caused by the atomic bomb at Nagasaki

bombed. Japan surrendered after the second explosion, when U.S. leaders agreed to allow the Japanese emperor to remain on his throne.

THE LEGACY OF WORLD WAR II

World War II was a global disaster of unprecedented dimensions. Over 50 million people lost their lives. Much of Europe, Africa, and Asia lay in ruins.

THE NUREMBERG TRIALS, 1945-1946

During the war, Hitler had murdered millions of European Jews and others in the **Holocaust**. The liberation of concentration camps revealed the full extent of Nazi brutality. The Allies put Nazi leaders on trial for "crimes against humanity" in Nuremberg, Germany. Those on trial claimed they were only following orders. Many were found guilty and were hanged or imprisoned. The Nuremberg Trials established that individuals are responsible if they commit atrocities, even during war.

THE OCCUPATION OF JAPAN

General **Douglas MacArthur**, who commanded the Allied forces in the Pacific, was assigned the task of rebuilding and reforming post-war Japan. Under his leadership, Japan's overseas empire was taken away, and military leaders were tried and punished. Japan renounced nuclear weapons and waging war. The country was forbidden from having a large army or navy. A new constitution in 1947 made Japan a democracy.

THE START OF THE COLD WAR, 1945-1960

The end of World War II left the United States and Soviet Union as two **superpowers** in command of the world. The U. S. had tremendous economic power and control of the atomic bomb. The Soviet Union had the world's largest army, which occupied most of Eastern Europe. Although allies during the war, these two superpowers soon became rivals in a "**Cold War**." The war was "cold" only in the sense that, because of nuclear weapons, the two superpowers never engaged one another in open warfare.

THE ROOTS OF THE COLD WAR

The roots of the Cold War lay in their competing ideological systems. The United States wanted to spread its democratic capitalist system. The Soviet Union wanted to spread its Communist system. It was inevitable that these superpowers would soon clash.

THE YALTA AND POTSDAM CONFERENCES

In early 1945, Roosevelt, Churchill and Stalin met at Yalta to plan for the reorganization of Europe after the war. They agreed to form the United Nations and to divide Germany into four separate occupation zones *(British, French, American, and Soviet)*. They also agreed to create democratic governments and to allow free elections in the countries they freed from German rule. Stalin pledged to allow free elections in Poland after the war. However, when Truman met with Stalin at the **Potsdam Conference** in Germany in 1945, serious differences emerged over Eastern Europe's future.

THE COLD WAR BEGINS

When Stalin refused to allow elections in Poland and Truman refused to share the secrets of the atomic bomb, the "Cold War" began in earnest. Instead of withdrawing, the Soviet army continued to occupy Eastern Europe. Stalin put Communist puppet goverments in power in all of Eastern Europe, making these countries Soviet "satellites." As if an "**Iron Curtain**" had fallen between Eastern and Western Europe, contact between the East and West was limited over the next forty years.

THE POLICY OF CONTAINMENT IN EUROPE

American leaders responded to the Soviet domination of Eastern Europe by developing the policy of **containment**. Under this policy, American leaders would not attempt to overturn Communism where it already existed, but resolved to prevent Communism from spreading to new areas.

THE BEGINNINGS OF CONTAINMENT

In 1947, when Communist rebels threatened Greece and Turkey, President Truman gave these countries military aid. Truman promised U.S. support to any country fighting Communism. This declaration, known as the **Truman Doctrine**, marked the beginning of America's containment policy. In 1948, Secretary of State **George Marshall** proposed that massive economic aid be given to the nations of Western Europe to rebuild their economies and reduce the attraction of Communism. Marshall believed this would create strong European allies for the United States. The **Marshall Plan** greatly speeded the economic recovery of Western Europe.

THE DIVISION OF GERMANY AND THE BERLIN AIRLIFT, 1948

In 1948, the French, British and Americans decided to merge their occupation zones into a single West German state. The Soviets reacted to this by announcing a blockade of West Berlin, closing all highway and railroad links to the West. The Western Allies refused to abandon Berlin, and began a massive airlift to feed and supply the city. Within a year, Stalin lifted the Soviet blockade.

THE FORMATION OF N.A.T.O. AND THE WARSAW PACT

The United States, Canada and ten Western European countries formed **NATO** (*North Atlantic Treaty Organization*) in 1949. Each NATO member pledged to defend every other member if attacked. Through NATO, the United States extended its umbrella of nuclear protection to Western Europe. The Soviet Union responded by creating the **Warsaw Pact** with its Eastern European satellites in 1955.

CONTAINMENT IN ASIA

Just when American leaders believed they had checked the spread of Communism in Europe, the world's most populous nation turned Communist in Asia. This raised a question: Could American leaders check the spread of Communism, not only in Europe, but everywhere on the globe?

CHINA FALLS TO COMMUNISM, 1949

In 1949, the Communists, led by **Mao Zedong**, defeated the Nationalist government. Mao then proceeded to create the world's largest Communist state. President Truman refused to recognize the Communist government in China. Using its veto power in the United Nations, the United States prevented admission of Mao's China to the U.N.

THE KOREAN WAR, 1950-1953

After World War II, Korea had been divided into two zones: in North Korea, the Soviets established a Communist government, while South Korea elected a non-Communist government. In 1950, North Korea invaded South Korea in an attempt to unify the country under Communist rule. President Truman saw this as similar to earlier Nazi aggression and ordered U.S. forces to South Korea to resist the invasion. When the Soviet Union boycotted the United Nations, the United States was able to pass a resolution authorizing the operation of U.N. troops in South Korea.

❖ **The Truman-MacArthur Controversy**. Truman sent General Douglas MacArthur to Korea to command U.N. forces. MacArthur landed his forces at Inchon. He then attacked North Korea, bringing the Chinese army into the war. MacArthur wanted to recapture China from the Communists, by using atomic weapons if needed. When Truman refused, MacArthur publicly criticized the President. Truman fired MacArthur, successfully asserting civilian control over the military.

❖ **The War Ends**. In 1952, **Dwight Eisenhower** was elected President after pledging that he would end the war in Korea. An armistice was signed that left Korea, with minor border adjustments, divided as it had been before the war.

THE NUCLEAR ARMS RACE BEGINS

By 1949, the Soviet Union had developed its own atomic bomb, starting a nuclear arms race. In 1952, the United States developed the hydrogen bomb, vastly more powerful than the atomic bomb. The Soviet Union exploded its first hydrogen bomb a year later, showing that the technology gap between the two superpowers was narrowing.

MASSIVE RETALIATION

Nuclear weapons acted as a **deterrent** — the Soviet Union would be *deterred* from attacking because if it did, the United States would destroy the Soviet Union with its nuclear weapons. The threat of massive retaliation cost less than a large conventional military force, but it was also less flexible. American leaders soon realized that in most situations nuclear weapons could not be used. Mass destruction could only be justified if the nation's survival were at stake.

MAJOR U.S. AND SOVIET MISSILE SITES

THE SOVIETS LAUNCH SPUTNIK

In 1957, the Soviet Union launched the first satellite, Sputnik, into space. It was clear that they were developing the ability to launch nuclear missiles that could strike the United States. This prompted the United States to send its own satellite into space in 1958, and the "Space Race" began.

EFFECTS OF THE COLD WAR ON U.S. SECURITY

As the Cold War grew more intense, Americans became very concerned with internal security. President Truman ordered the establishment of **Loyalty Review Boards** to investigate individual "un-American" acts, such as participation in organizations like the American Communist Party. Congress conducted its own loyalty checks through the House Un-American Activities Committee.

THE ROSENBERG TRIALS

In 1950, **Julius and Ethel Rosenberg** were indicted for selling secret information about the atomic bomb to the Soviet Union. The Rosenbergs were executed for treason, even though many Americans had doubts about their guilt.

THE MCCARTHY HEARINGS

In 1950, Senator **Joseph McCarthy** shocked the nation by claiming to know the names of many Communists who had infiltrated the State Department and the U.S. Army. McCarthy eventually lost his influence when he could produce no evidence during Congressional hearings. The term **McCarthyism** has come to mean making wild accusations without proof. McCarthyism showed the extent of anxiety caused by the Cold War.

CHECKING YOUR UNDERSTANDING

KEY TERMS AND CONCEPTS

Make a vocabulary card for each of the following terms and concepts.

- ✦ Isolationism
- ✦ Appeasement
- ✦ Neutrality Acts
- ✦ Lend-Lease Act

- ✦ *Korematsu v. U.S.*
- ✦ Nuremberg Trials.
- ✦ Iron Curtain
- ✦ Cold War

- ✦ Truman Doctrine
- ✦ Marshall Plan
- ✦ Korean War
- ✦ McCarthyism

MULTIPLE-CHOICE QUESTIONS

1   Which was an example of appeasement?
   1   the U. S. Neutrality Acts of 1935 and 1937
   2   the conquest of Poland in 1939
   3   the agreement at Munich in 1938 to give Germany the Sudetenland
   4   American entry into World War II

2   Between World War I and World War II, the United States followed a policy of
   1   isolation from European military conflicts
   2   containment of Communism
   3   active membership in the League of Nations
   4   military alliances with France and Great Britain

3   Which group of American citizens experienced the greatest loss of constitutional rights during a period of U.S. military involvement?
   1   Hispanic Americans during the Spanish-American War
   2   German Americans during World War I
   3   Japanese Americans during World War II
   4   Chinese Americans during the Korean conflict

4   The bombing of Hiroshima and Nagasaki resulted in
   1   the outbreak of World War II
   2   U.S. entry into the war against Japan
   3   the surrender of Japan
   4   a decrease in the spread of Communism

5   Which was a major result of World War II?
   1   Great Britain and France helped rebuild the Soviet Union.
   2   Japan gained an empire in mainland Asia.
   3   Germany gained control of Eastern Europe.
   4   Germany was divided into zones of occupation.

6   Which fundamental principle was expressed by the war crimes tribunal at Nuremberg?
     1   National leaders are responsible for their wartime actions.
     2   National policies during wartime cannot be criticized after a war.
     3   Individuals acting for their nation cannot be prosecuted for their actions.
     4   The use of nuclear weapons is never justified.

7   The term "Cold War" refers to
     1   U.S. neutrality in the early years of World War II
     2   Prime Minister Chamberlain's attempts to appease Hitler
     3   the border dispute between the Soviet Union and Communist China
     4   a long period of hostility between the United States and the Soviet Union

8   A study of the Red Scare (1920s) and McCarthyism (1950s) shows that
     1   many Communists infiltrated high levels of the federal government
     2   fears of disloyalty can lead to the erosion of constitutional freedoms
     3   Communism gains influence in times of economic recession
     4   loyalty oaths by government employees prevent espionage

THEMATIC ESSAY QUESTION

Directions: Write a well-organized essay that includes an introduction, several paragraphs explaining your position, and a conclusion.

Theme: Foreign Policy

> The U. S. has pursued a variety of foreign policy goals to advance its vital interests.

Task:

> Choose **two** foreign policy goals from your study of American history.
>
> For *each* foreign policy goal:
> * *Describe* the foreign policy identified.
> * *Describe* an action taken by the U.S. in pursuit of that foreign policy goal.

You may use any example from your study of U.S. history. Some suggestions you might wish to consider include: purchase of the Louisiana Territory from France (1803), declaration of war on Spain (1898), acquisition of colonies during the Progressive Era (late 1800s), building of the Panama Canal (1903), entry into World War I (1917), entry into World War II (1941), and the containment of Communism (1947-1953).

You are *not* limited to these suggestions

DOCUMENT-BASED ESSAY QUESTION

This question is based on the accompanying documents (1-7). This question is designed to test your ability to work with historical documents. Some of the documents have been edited for the purposes of the question. As you analyze the documents, take into account both the source of each document and any point of view that may be presented in the document.

Historical Context: As a result of the Progressive Era, the New Deal, and two world wars, the power of the federal government expanded tremendously between 1900 and 1950.

Task: Using information from the documents and your knowledge of U.S. history, answer the questions that follow each document in Part A. Your answers to the questions will help you write the Part B essay, in which you will be asked to:

> Evaluate the expansion of federal government power in the first half of the twentieth century by comparing its advantages and disadvantages.

Part A — Short Answer Questions

Directions: Analyze the documents and answer the short-answer questions that follow each document in the space provided.

Document 1:

SELECTED FEDERAL LEGISLATION

ACT	DESCRIPTION
Pure Food and Drug Act (1906)	Banned the manufacture and sale of impure foods and drugs, and required medicines to be truthfully labeled.
Federal Reserve Act (1913)	Established the Federal Reserve System to regulate the nation's money supply.
Income Tax (1913)	First direct federal tax on citizens' incomes, permitted by the Sixteenth Amendment to the Constitution.
National Labor Relations Act (1934)	Established the National Labor Relations Board to enforce the right of workers to organize into unions.
Social Security Act (1935)	Provided workers with federal unemployment insurance and old age pensions, paid for by a tax on wages.

1a. What do all of these federal acts have in common? _____

1b. What trend in the role of government is indicated by this chart? _____

Document 2:

> *"I insisted that the executive power was limited only by specific restrictions and prohibitions in the Constitution or imposed by Congress. My view was that every executive officer in high position was a steward of the people. I refused to accept the view that what was necessary for the nation could not be done by the President unless he could find some specific authorization to do it."*
>
> — Theodore Roosevelt, on Presidential power, 1913

2. What did Roosevelt see as the main limits on the expansion of Presidential power?

_____

Document 3:

> *"My view of the executive function is that the President can exercise no power which cannot be reasonably traced to some specific grant of power or implied as proper and necessary to its exercise. Such a specific grant must be either in the federal Constitution or an act of Congress. There is no undefined power which he can exercise because it seems to him to be in the public interest."*
>
> — President William Howard Taft , 1916

3. In what way did Taft view Presidential power as limited? _____

Document 4:

> *"If somebody puts a derrick improperly on top of a building, then the government has the right to see that derrick is so secure that you can walk under it and not be afraid that it is going to fall. Likewise, it is the privilege of the government to see that human life is protected, that human lungs have something to breathe ... The first duty of law is to keep sound the society it serves."*
>
> — President Woodrow Wilson, 1916

4 Why did Wilson reject the idea of a laissez-faire role for government?_____

Document 5:

> *"There are an additional 3.5 million people who are on relief. This group was the victim of a depression caused by conditions which were not local but national. The federal government is the only government with sufficient power to meet this situation. We have assumed this task. It is the duty of national policy to give employment to these people, pending their absorption by private employment.*
>
> — President Franklin D. Roosevelt, 1935

5. What did Roosevelt argue was the responsibility of the federal government in the face of widespread national unemployment? _____

Document 6:

6. What is the cartoonist's view of Roosevelt's New Deal?

Library of Congress

_____

_____

_____

Document 7:

> "We have seen these gigantic expenditures and this torrent of waste pile up a national debt which two generations cannot repay. We have seen the increase of political officials. We have seen the pressures on the destitute to trade political support for relief. Both pollute foundations of liberty... Either we shall have a society based on liberty and the initiative of the individual, or we shall have a planned society that means dictation, no matter what you call it ."
>
> — Former President Herbert Hoover on the New Deal, 1936

7. Why did Hoover believe that the federal government was becoming dangerously powerful under the New Deal? _____

Part B — Essay

Directions:

• Write a well-organized essay that includes an introduction, several paragraphs, and a conclusion.

• Use evidence from at least **four** documents to support your response.

• Include additional related information.

Historical Context: As a result of the Progressive Era, the New Deal, and two world wars, the power of the federal government expanded tremendously between 1900 and 1950.

Task:

Using information from the documents and your knowledge of U.S. history, write an essay in which you:

> Evaluate the expansion of federal government power in the first half of the twentieth century by comparing its advantages and disadvantages.

CHAPTER 10

THE WORLD IN UNCERTAIN TIMES

The 1950s and 1960s were a time of prosperity and social reform, in which our present-day pluralistic society was forged. After World War II, Americans enjoyed the benefits of their new standing as a military and economic superpower. However, this period was also a time of social change. The Civil Rights Movement sought equality for African Americans; the Women's Liberation Movement strove to achieve greater rights for women; Presidents Kennedy and Johnson introduced programs to help the poor; and an activist Supreme Court expanded individual rights. This reform period was brought to a close by the Vietnam War. In this chapter you will learn about:

Dr. Martin Luther King, Jr.

- **The Civil Rights Movement**. African Americans ended racial segregation in public schools and other public places, and obtained equal civil rights.

- **The Post-War Presidents**. President Kennedy introduced a new style to the Presidency, but was assassinated in 1963. President Johnson introduced his "Great Society" programs to help the poor.

- **The Sixties**: The 1960s saw a new rebelliousness among young people, women demanding greater equality, and a growing militancy among African Americans. The Supreme Court issued important rulings protecting individual rights.

- **The War in Vietnam**. The United States became involved in defending the government of South Vietnam from Communist attack. Despite sending massive aid and half a million troops, the United States was unable to win the war. The Vietnam War was one of the most divisive conflicts in U.S. history.

In studying this period, you should focus on the following questions:

✦ What were the achievements of the Civil Rights Movement?
✦ What factors led to the Women's Liberation Movement?
✦ How did Johnson's "Great Society" attempt to achieve social reform?
✦ What were the effects of the war in Vietnam?

THE CIVIL RIGHTS MOVEMENT

One of the most important developments of the 1950s and 1960s was the struggle for equal rights by African Americans. The United States had once held out the promise of equality to African Americans at the end of the Civil War, but this promise had been cut short in the aftermath of Reconstruction. In 1947, **Jackie Robinson** became the first African-American baseball player to cross the "color line" and join the major leagues. The next year, President Truman signed an executive order to desegregate the armed forces and end racial discrimination in the hiring practices of the federal government.

Jackie Robinson

Schomberg Center for Black Culture

BROWN V. BOARD OF EDUCATION, 1954

The Supreme Court's decision in *Brown v. Board of Education* was central to the emergence of the Civil Rights Movement in the 1950s and 1960s.

BACKGROUND

In *Plessy v. Ferguson*, the Supreme Court had upheld the constitutionality of segregation laws. N.A.A.C.P. lawyers began challenging this "**separate-but-equal**" doctrine. In 1953, they appealed a Kansas court ruling where an African-American student had been denied admission to an all-white public school near her home. The N.A.A.C.P. argued that segregated public schools denied African-American children the "equal protection" of the law guaranteed to them under the Fourteenth Amendment. They argued that the separate education received by African-American students was inferior by its very nature, since it implied they were not good enough to be educated with other students.

THE DECISION

Chief Justice **Earl Warren** wrote the unanimous decision. The Supreme Court ruled that segregation in public schools was unconstitutional: "Separate-but-equal has no place in the field of public education. Separate educational facilities are inherently unequal." The Court ruled that segregation should be ended "with all due deliberate speed." Nevertheless, it took years before the *Brown* decision was fully carried out.

THE MARCH TO EQUALITY

Dr. Martin Luther King, Jr. emerged in the late 1950s as the main leader of the Civil Rights Movement. Like Henry David Thoreau and Mohandas Gandhi before him, King believed in **non-violence** — that passive resistance to unjust laws could change the attitudes of oppressors. King carried out this resistance through **civil disobedience** — if the government passed an unjust law, people should oppose it with non-violent tactics such as boycotts, picketing, sit-ins and demonstrations.

THE MONTGOMERY BUS BOYCOTT, 1955-1956

Rosa Parks was arrested for not giving up her seat on a bus to a white passenger in Montgomery, Alabama. Her arrest inspired local black leaders to begin a 13-month boycott of Montgomery's public buses, eventually resulting in their desegregation. The boycott showed that African Americans could unite successfully to oppose segregation.

LITTLE ROCK, ARKANSAS, 1957

In Arkansas, the governor refused to provide special protection to nine black students attending an all-white high school in Little Rock. These students were being threatened by angry mobs. President Eisenhower ordered federal troops to Little Rock to ensure that the students could attend the school.

SIT-INS AND FREEDOM RIDES IN THE SOUTH, 1960-1961

In 1960, African-American students held a "sit-in" at a "Whites Only" lunch counter in North Carolina. The tactic was soon copied throughout the South by students who supported the Civil Rights Movement. In 1961, interracial groups rode interstate and local buses in **Freedom Rides** through the South. These Freedom Riders sought to create confrontations in the hope that the federal government would intervene.

THE MARCH ON WASHINGTON, 1963

In 1963, Dr. King and other Civil Rights leaders called for a **March on Washington** in support of a new Civil Rights bill pending in Congress. A quarter of a million people attended the march. King gave his famous "I Have A Dream" speech, in which he looked forward to the day when Americans of all colors would live together peacefully.

CIVIL RIGHTS ACT OF 1964

In 1964, President Johnson was able to push a bill through Congress. The bill prohibited discrimination based on race, religion, or ethnic origin in hotels and in places of employment doing business with the federal government. The act cut off federal money to districts with segregated schools. In addition, the federal government was given power to register voters and to establish a commission to enforce the act.

THE STRUGGLE TO ACHIEVE VOTING RIGHTS

After passage of the **Civil Rights Act of 1964,** Civil Rights leaders turned their energies to registering black voters and encouraging them to vote. The **Twenty-fourth
Amendment** (1964) eliminated poll taxes in federal elections. The following year, the
Voting Rights Act (1965) ended poll taxes and suspended literacy tests where they
were being used to prevent African Americans from voting.

AFFIRMATIVE ACTION, 1965

In 1965, President Johnson signed an executive order requiring employers with federal
contracts to raise the number of their minority and female employees to correct past
imbalances. **Affirmative action** programs also increased minority representation in
colleges and the professions. Although this was upheld by the Supreme Court in *University of California v. Bakke* (1978), many affirmative action programs have been
phased out over time as America has moved towards a more pluralistic society.

THE POST-WAR PRESIDENTS: EISENHOWER, KENNEDY AND JOHNSON

THE EISENHOWER YEARS, 1953-1960

In addition to witnessing the beginning of the Civil Rights Movement, the 1950s were
a period of recovery and economic growth. President Eisenhower's years in office were
marked by several important developments.

DOMESTIC DEVELOPMENTS DURING THE EISENHOWER PRESIDENCY

Housing Boom. This was a time of high birth rates, known as the "baby boom." This boom and the G.I. Bill, which helped veterans get mortgages, led developers to build cheaper, mass-produced housing. Home ownership increased by 50%.

Prosperity. The demand for consumer goods reached all-time highs. Millions of autos and TV sets were sold. The use of refrigerators and other appliances became widespread. The gross domestic product doubled from 1945 to 1960. America dominated world trade.

Conformity. In the late 1950s, there was a greater emphasis on conformity. Unusual ideas were regarded with suspicion. Fear of Communism strengthened the dislike of non-conformist attitudes.

THE KENNEDY PRESIDENCY, 1960-1963

In 1960, John F. Kennedy was elected President. As part of his **New Frontier**, Kennedy proposed a tax cut to stimulate the economy, the creation of Medicare, civil rights legislation, and increased aid to education. Only the tax cut was passed by Congress. One of the greatest challenges Kennedy faced was the establishment of a Communist government by Fidel Castro in Cuba, only 90 miles from Florida.

❖ **Bay of Pigs Invasion**. In 1961, Cuban exiles, trained in the United States, invaded Cuba at the Bay of Pigs. Kennedy, fearing **Soviet** involvement, refused to give them air support and they were defeated by Castro's army. This was a major foreign policy failure for the Kennedy Administration.

❖ **Cuban Missile Crisis**. In 1962, the United States discovered that Cuba was secretly trying to build bases for Soviet nuclear missiles. Kennedy imposed a naval blockade on Cuba and threatened to invade if the missiles were not withdrawn. For several days the world stood on the brink of nuclear war. Soviet leader Khrushchev agreed to withdraw the missiles for a pledge that the United States would not invade Cuba.

Soviet missile launching site in Cuba (spy photo)

THE JOHNSON PRESIDENCY, 1963-1968

The nation was shocked when Kennedy was assassinated on November 22, 1963 while visiting Dallas, Texas. Vice President **Lyndon Johnson** was immediately sworn in as the next President. As President, Johnson proposed to Congress the most far-ranging social legislation since the New Deal. Johnson's aim was to turn the United States into a **"Great Society"** by opening up opportunities for all citizens and improving the quality of American life.

Civil Rights. Johnson passed a broad program of civil rights legislation, such as the **Civil Rights Acts** (1964) and the **Voting Rights Act** (1965).

Aid to Cities. Money was provided for urban planning, slum clearance, rental assistance for the poor, and the reconstruction of buildings.

JOHNSON'S GREAT SOCIETY PROGRAMS

Medicare Act of 1965. Social Security was expanded to provide medical care, hospital insurance, and post-hospital nursing for people over age 65.

War on Poverty. Johnson called for a "war on poverty." He created new programs to help the poor, such as the **Job Corps** to train underprivileged youths, and a domestic "**Peace Corps**" to help in depressed areas.

THE GREAT SOCIETY AND THE VIETNAM WAR

Despite these Great Society programs, many Americans remained in poverty. The high cost of spending caused by U.S. involvement in the Vietnam War eventually forced Johnson to withdraw much of the funding for his new domestic programs.

THE SIXTIES: A DECADE OF CHANGE

The 1960s and early 1970s, many groups became more militant in their demand for a more equal and diverse American society.

THE YOUTH CULTURE OF THE SIXTIES

In the 1960s and 1970s, many young people adopted a spirit of rebelliousness. They challenged the materialism of those in charge of American society. They were shocked at the Establishment's indifference to poverty and other problems. The new "**youth culture**" experimented openly with drugs and sex. They adopted new fashions to set them apart from traditional styles. In the late 1960s, many youths focused on American involvement in Vietnam. By 1968, millions of young people were actively protesting the war. Protests continued until the United States withdrew from the war in 1973.

Protesters burn their draft cards to show their opposition to the war

THE WOMEN'S LIBERATION MOVEMENT

Another of the important events of the 1960s was the Women's Liberation, or **Feminist Movement**. Unlike the earlier Suffrage Movement, which focused on securing the vote, the **Women's Liberation Movement** of the 1960s was directed at achieving economic and social equality.

EMERGENCE OF THE WOMEN'S LIBERATION MOVEMENT

Many women were dissatisfied with their roles as housewives and sought to express themselves in careers and work. Feminists such as **Betty Freidan** provided leadership. Her book *The Feminine Mystique* revealed the frustration many women felt at being restricted to homemaking and motherhood. Sex education courses began to be taught in the schools. Birth control pills protected women from pregnancy.

ACCOMPLISHMENTS OF THE WOMEN'S LIBERATION MOVEMENT

As a result of affirmative action, universities could no longer discriminate on the basis of gender in their admissions policy. As a result, colleges became co-educational and hired women professors. Gender equality was achieved in military academies (*West Point and Annapolis*) and in law and medical schools. In 1963, Congress passed the **"Equal Pay" Act** requiring companies to pay women the same as men for the same work. Feminists introduced the title Ms. to replace Miss and Mrs. They opposed sexist language (*"policeman" and "fireman"*) and textbooks that ignored women's contributions to society. They lobbied Congress for more funds to research women's diseases.

THE ABORTION ISSUE

Many states had laws banning abortion. Feminists believed that women should have the right to choose whether or not to have an abortion. "Pro-choice" rights became a rallying cry for the Women's Movement. The issue became one of the most divisive in American history. In 1973, the Supreme Court ruled in **Roe v. Wade** that women's constitutional right to privacy guaranteed the right to an abortion in early pregnancy.

INCREASING AFRICAN-AMERICAN MILITANCY

The demand for change was particularly strong among young African Americans who believed progress was not being achieved fast enough. In the North, African Americans faced segregation based on residential living patterns. Many were confined to inner cities. In 1968, Martin Luther King was assassinated. For three summers, rioters in cities across the nation smashed windows, overturned cars, and began fires. The **Kerner Commission**, investigating the unrest, found the lack of job opportunities for African Americans, urban poverty and racism to be the chief factors behind the riots.

The militants believed in **Black Power.** New groups challenged traditional, non-violent organizations like the N.A.A.C.P. **Black Panthers** demanded reparations for centuries of discrimination. **Black Muslims** believed African Americans should have their own state. **Malcolm X**, a Black Muslim, argued for meeting violence with violence, but he moderated his views after a pilgrimage to Mecca. He urged blacks to control their own communities. He was assassinated by rival Muslims in 1965.

Malcom X giving a speech

NATIVE AMERICAN INDIANS BECOME MILITANT

The Civil Rights Act banned discrimination against Native American Indians. In 1970, President Nixon announced the government would honor its treaty obligations, but many tribes still felt mistreated. Under the slogan "**Red Power**," they formed the **American Indian Movement**(A.I.M.). Their leaders sought respect for the Indian heritage. They introduced the term "Native American" and protested racial biases and stereotypes against their ethnic group. To bring attention to their cause, they temporarily occupied government property like Alcatraz Island in California.

THE WARREN COURT

Under Chief Justice **Earl Warren**, the Supreme Court became a major instrument of social change — protecting individual rights, minority groups and those accused of crimes.

❖ **Mapp v. Ohio**, 1961. The Supreme Court ruled that evidence obtained by the police through an illegal search could not be used in court.

❖ **Baker v. Carr**, 1962. Under legislative districting in some states, rural areas were over-represented and cities were under-represented. The Court ruled these legislative districts must be reapportioned on the basis of "one man, one vote."

❖ **Gideon v. Wainwright**, 1963. The Court ruled that states must provide a free lawyer to any criminal defendant facing imprisonment who could not afford one.

❖ **Miranda v. Arizona**, 1966. A man confessed to a rape without being informed that he could have a lawyer present. The Court overturned his conviction, ruling that the police must inform suspects of their "Miranda" rights: to remain silent, to have a lawyer present during questioning, and that what they say can be used against them.

THE VIETNAM WAR, 1954-1973

The "decade of change" ended with Americans deeply divided over the **Vietnam War**. Vietnam was once a French colony in Indochina. In 1954, the Vietnamese defeated the French. At the **Geneva Conference** that followed, Vietnam was divided into two. The country was to be reunited after elections were held in 1956. South Vietnamese leaders later refused to hold the elections, however, since they feared elections in the North would not be free. South Vietnamese Communists (**Vietcong**), with North Vietnamese support, began a guerrilla war against the government of South Vietnam.

THE WAR UNDER PRESIDENT KENNEDY, 1960-1963

Kennedy, responding to requests from the South Vietnamese government for help, sent aid and 16,000 military advisers to train the Vietnamese army to fight the Vietcong. U.S. leaders believed in the **domino theory**: they thought if South Vietnam fell to Communism, other Southeast Asian countries might also fall, like a row of dominos.

THE WAR UNDER PRESIDENT JOHNSON, 1963-1968

In 1964, Johnson announced that the North Vietnamese had attacked U.S. ships in the Gulf of Tonkin. Congress gave the President power to stop this aggression. Johnson used the **Gulf of Tonkin Resolution** to escalate the war, ordering massive bombing raids of North Vietnam. He also sent more combat troops to South Vietnam. Despite the large American force, the Vietcong launched the **Tet Offensive** in South Vietnam in 1968, seizing many cities. This convinced Americans that victory was far off. The war grew increasingly unpopular, and opponents held demonstrations and rallies.

THE WAR UNDER PRESIDENT NIXON, 1969-1973

During Nixon's term the war dragged on for five more years. Under his "Vietnamization" policy, the South Vietnamese army gradually took over the brunt of fighting, allowing U.S. forces to gradually withdraw. In 1973, Nixon's negotiators in Paris worked out a cease-fire agreement with the North Vietnamese. After the U.S. withdrew, fighting continued. South Vietnam fell to Communist forces in 1975, and Vietnam was reunited under Communist rule. After the war, Congress passed the **War Powers Act** (1973) which limited the President's power to involve the nation in armed conflict without a formal declaration of war by Congress. The act required the President to inform Congress within 48 hours of sending troops to fight overseas. If within 60 days Congress did not approve the use of these forces, the President must withdraw the troops.

CHECKING YOUR UNDERSTANDING

KEY TERMS AND CONCEPTS

Make a vocabulary card for each of the following terms and concepts.

+ *Brown v. Board of Education*
+ March on Washington
+ Affirmative Action

+ Bay of Pigs Invasion
+ Cuban Missile Crisis
+ Great Society

+ War on Poverty
+ "Domino Theory"
+ War Powers Act

MULTIPLE-CHOICE QUESTIONS

1   In *Brown v. Board of Education*, the Supreme Court ruled that
   1   busing children to overcome segregation is constitutional
   2   racially segregated public schools are unconstitutional
   3   the use of civil disobedience to achieve legal rights is constitutional
   4   delaying integration to avoid violence is constitutional

2   Which statement is best illustrated by the Supreme Court decision in *Brown v. Board of Education?*
   1   The Constitution ensures federal control of state academic requirements.
   2   Racial prejudice no longer exists in the United States.
   3   Non-whites have gained economic and political equality with whites.
   4   The Court's interpretation of the Constitution may change over time.

3   Which development was a result of the other three?
   1   African Americans were barred from voting in several states.
   2   State laws supported racial segregation in schools and housing.
   3   The Civil Rights and Voting Rights Acts were passed.
   4   Civil Rights advocates held boycotts, demonstrations and sit-ins.

4   With which statement would a follower of Martin Luther King, Jr. most likely agree?
   1   All properly enacted laws must be obeyed.
   2   Demonstrations against unfair laws are morally justified.
   3   Civil disobedience is damaging to society.
   4   Violence is acceptable if the cause is just.

5   Which action best illustrates affirmative action?
   1   A company actively recruits qualified women and minority members.
   2   A corporation hires people on a "first come, first serve" basis.
   3   A university's sole criterion for admission is its entrance examination.
   4   A graduate school accepts all students who apply.

6 Malcolm X and Martin Luther King, Jr. chiefly disagreed over the
  1 use of violence to achieve equality   3 issue of U.S. aid to Africa
  2 desirability of racial equality   4 degree of pride in being black

7 The terms "hippies," "youth culture," "anti-establishment" would most likely be used in an essay dealing with which decade?
  1 the 1940s   3 the 1960s
  2 the 1950s   4 the 1980s

8 In *Roe v. Wade*, the Supreme Court ruled that
  1 racial segregation in public schools is unconstitutional
  2 the Court has the power to declare federal laws unconstitutional
  3 women deserve equal pay for equal work
  4 the right to privacy allows women to have abortions in early pregnancy

9 The primary purpose of the War Powers Act of 1973 was to
  1 limit Presidential power to send troops into combat
  2 encourage a quicker response to a military attack
  3 assure adequate defense of the Western Hemisphere
  4 prevent the use of troops for non-military purposes

THEMATIC ESSAY QUESTION

Directions: Write a well-organized essay that includes an introduction, several paragraphs explaining your position, and a conclusion.

Theme: Human Rights

> Many U.S. Supreme Court decisions have dealt with important issues and had a major impact on American society.

Task:

> Select **two** Supreme Court cases from your study of American history.
>
> For *each* Supreme Court case:
> * *Explain how* the Supreme Court case dealt with an important issue
> * *Discuss* its impact on American society.

You may use any example from your study of American history. Some suggestions you might wish to consider include: *Dred Scott v. Sandford, Korematsu v. U.S., Brown v. Board of Education, Miranda v. Arizona,* and *Roe v. Wade.*

You are *not* limited to these suggestions.

CHAPTER 11

CONTEMPORARY AMERICA

Many new developments occurred during the past thirty years. Under President Nixon, the U.S. withdrew from Vietnam and opened diplomatic relations with Communist China. In the 1970s, the nation experienced recession and inflation. U.S. prestige suffered when American hostages were held in Iran for over a year. Under Presidents Reagan and Bush, America moved toward greater conservatism in government. Under President Clinton, Americans enjoyed unparalleled prosperity. In this chapter you will learn about:

The White House

President Bush (at right) meets with Russian President Boris Yeltsin

- **The Presidency in Crisis**. Under Nixon, the Watergate scandal weakened the prestige of the Presidency. Presidents Ford and Carter had to deal with rising oil prices, economic recession, and new acts of aggression by the Soviet Union.

- **The Trend Toward Conservatism**. President Reagan cut domestic spending, restored prosperity, and aided anti-Communist rebels, but the national debt soared. Bush followed similar policies and witnessed the end of the Cold War.

- **The United States Today**. Under President Clinton, the United States experienced great economic prosperity. As the only remaining superpower, the nation searched for a new role in promoting international stability and justice.

- **Toward a Post-Industrial World**. Recent technological, economic and environmental developments and choices will shape our future.

In studying this period, you should focus on the following questions:

✦ How have recent Presidents coped with domestic problems and encouraged prosperity?
✦ How well have recent Presidents protected U.S. interests in foreign affairs?
✦ What changes can Americans expect in the future?

THE PRESIDENCY IN CRISIS

Presidential power had greatly increased as a result of the New Deal and two World Wars. The Cold War made the President's role even more important. Under Presidents Nixon, Ford, and Carter, many wondered whether the Presidency had become overwhelming — with greater responsibility than one person could handle effectively.

THE NIXON PRESIDENCY, 1969-1974

Nixon believed that federal social programs were often inefficient, and that most social problems were best dealt with at the local level. Under his policy of **New Federalism,** Nixon reversed the trend of increasing federal control by turning over some federal tax revenues to state governments. The early 1970s saw rising inflation. Nixon cut spending on social programs and imposed wage and price controls. These attempts to control inflation proved unsuccessful.

President Nixon delivers his inaugural address in January, 1969

FOREIGN POLICY UNDER NIXON

Nixon believed the President's major role was to direct the country's foreign policy. As we have seen, Nixon's policy of "Vietnamization" shifted the fighting from American troops to the South Vietnamese. In 1973, Nixon agreed to the **Paris Peace Accords,** and U.S. troops were withdrawn from Vietnam. Ever since the Communist Revolution in China in 1949, U.S. leaders had refused to establish diplomatic relations with the Chinese. Instead, they treated the Nationalist Chinese government on Taiwan as the official government of China. Nixon finally visited mainland China and restored diplomatic relations with the Chinese. Nixon also introduced **détente** — a relaxing of strained relations — with the Soviet Union. In 1972, Nixon visited Moscow and signed the **SALT I Accord,** which limited the development of certain types of missile systems.

THE WATERGATE CRISIS

In 1973 **Spiro Agnew** resigned as Vice President when it was discovered he had taken bribes while serving as Governor of Maryland. Under the **Twenty-fifth Amendment,**

Nixon appointed Congressman Gerald Ford to replace Agnew as Vice-President. In 1972, a group of former CIA agents, working for Nixon's re-election, were caught breaking into Democratic Party headquarters at the Watergate complex in Washington, D.C. Nixon tried to cover up an investigation of the break-in on the grounds of national security. In Senate hearings, it was revealed that Nixon secretly recorded all his White House conversations. When the Senate Committee asked to hear the tapes, Nixon refused, claiming **executive privilege**. The Supreme Court ruled that Nixon must turn over the tapes, reaffirming the principle that no one is above the law. The tapes revealed that Nixon had lied when he said he was not involved in the cover-up. Fearing impeachment, Nixon became the first President ever to resign.

THE FORD PRESIDENCY, 1974-1977

Gerald Ford

Bureau of Engraving and Printing

Gerald Ford, an unelected Vice President, became the next President. One of Ford's first acts was to pardon Nixon for any crimes he had committed. This caused severe public criticism. As President, Ford's main worries were over the economy. The nation suffered from **stagflation** — high unemployment because of a stagnant economy, and high inflation. The problem was caused by the reduction in government defense spending after the Vietnam War and by drastic increases in international oil prices. In 1975 South Vietnam finally fell to the Communists. Ford had asked Congress for funds to try to save the South Vietnamese government, but Congress refused. Ford continued Nixon's policy of détente with the Soviet Union. In 1975, the U.S., the Soviet Union and other nations signed the **Helsinki Accords**, recognizing post-World War II borders and pledging to respect human rights.

THE CARTER PRESIDENCY, 1977-1981

Democrat **Jimmy Carter** was elected as an "outsider" who promised to clean up Washington. Like Ford, Carter's chief problems were economic. The U.S. was heavily dependent on imported oil. As oil prices skyrocketed, inflation went over 10%, interest rates rose to 20%, and unemployment grew. To deal with the crisis, Carter created the Department of Energy and increased the nation's fuel reserves. Carter sought a special tax on large automobiles and the power to ration gasoline, but Congress refused. High oil prices and shortages continued throughout the Carter years. Carter cut federal spending, but inflation did not come down until two years into the Reagan Presidency.

FOREIGN POLICY

Carter made human rights a high priority: he condemned apartheid in South Africa, pressured the Soviet Union to allow Jews to emigrate, and cut aid to dictatorships that violated human rights.

President Carter addresses Congress

❖ **The Panama Canal Treaty**, 1977. Carter signed a treaty returning the Panama Canal to Panama in 1999.

❖ **The Camp David Accords**. In 1977, Carter invited Egypt's President Sadat and Israel's Prime Minister Begin to Camp David, where an agreement was reached. Israel returned the Sinai Peninsula to Egypt in exchange for a peace treaty and the establishment of normal relations.

❖ **The Iranian Revolution and the Hostage Crisis** (1978-1979). The Shah of Iran was a brutal dictator, but also a U.S. ally. In 1978, widespread demonstrations broke out against the Shah. When he fled the country, religious leaders hostile to Western influences seized control. They resented America for helping the Shah and backing Israel. In retaliation, Iranian students seized the staff of the U.S. embassy in Iran, holding them hostage for 444 days. Negotiations finally led to their release, but only on the day Ronald Reagan became President.

THE NEW CONSERVATISM: THE REAGAN AND BUSH PRESIDENCIES

Under Presidents Reagan and Bush, the federal government moved in a conservative direction — reducing social spending and cutting federal regulations, while involving itself more aggressively in foreign affairs.

THE REAGAN PRESIDENCY, 1981-1989

Carter was defeated by **Ronald Reagan** in the Presidential election of 1980. Reagan believed strongly that individuals and businesses were better able to solve economic problems than the government was. Reagan supported the policy of **New Federalism** first begun under President Nixon.

Library of Congress

DOMESTIC POLICY

Reagan tried to solve stagflation with **supply-side economics**. He believed a large supply of goods would decrease prices and stop inflation. Under "**Reaganomics**," he cut taxes on businesses and the wealthy. He felt these groups would invest their tax savings to raise productivity and increase employment, resulting in benefits that would "trickle down" to other groups. To finance the tax cut, Reagan reduced spending on welfare and disability programs. He also eliminated many regulations on industry. Reagan increased military spending, which he financed by borrowing. This spending stimulated the economy, but led to an increased federal deficit and doubled the national debt.

Reagan proved to be one of the nation's most popular Presidents

FOREIGN POLICY

Reagan set out to rebuild American confidence in the aftermath of Vietnam and Watergate. He believed that the United States should continue to act as the world's defender of freedom and democracy. In 1983, Reagan sent U.S. Marines to the island of **Grenada** to defeat Communists who had taken control. The action showed Reagan's willingness to use force to protect Americans on the island and to prevent the Soviet Union from exporting Communism to countries in the Western Hemisphere. To carry out this new foreign policy, Reagan sharply increased military spending.

❖ **The Iran-Contra Affair**. In 1986, President Reagan announced the **Reagan Doctrine** — the U.S. would no longer just contain Communism, but would roll it back by aiding anti-Communist "freedom fighters." Under this policy, the Reagan Administration secretly sold arms to Iran. Profits from the sale were used to support the "Contra" rebels fighting the Communist government of Nicaragua, even though Congress had passed a law forbidding aid to the Contras. An investigation cleared the President but led to several Reagan officials being sent to prison.

❖ **Democracy Triumphs**. The last years of Reagan's Presidency saw the beginning of an end to the Cold War. The economic failures of Communism forced Soviet leaders to introduce new reforms. Soviet leader **Mikhail Gorbachev** agreed to withdraw troops from Afghanistan and to allow a peaceful transition to democracy in Eastern Europe. Reagan and Gorbachev held a series of summit conferences, and signed an agreement to dismantle thousands of nuclear missiles.

THE GEORGE H.W. BUSH PRESIDENCY, 1989 - 1993

Reagan's Vice President, **George H.W. Bush**, campaigned in the 1988 election on a promise to continue Reagan's policies, but with an emphasis on improving education, fighting drug use, and greater compassion for the poor and the disadvantaged. In 1990, Bush signed the **Americans with Disabilities Act** prohibiting discrimination against people with disabilities in the areas of employment and public accommodations. Bush's greatest domestic challenge was to reduce the growing budget deficit. He was blamed when the nation slipped into a recession in 1990.

FOREIGN POLICY

Bush proved more successful in his foreign policy initiatives. In 1989, Bush sent U.S. forces to Panama against the drug-dealing dictator **Manuel Noriega**. Noriega was taken to the United States and convicted on drug charges. However, the most important event of the Bush Presidency was the end of the Cold War. From 1989 to 1991, Eastern Europe moved from Communism to democracy, the Berlin Wall was torn down, and East and West Germany were reunited. Gorbachev's reforms set in motion a series of events that, by 1991, led to the collapse of the Soviet Union and its replacement by the Commonwealth of Independent States.

THE GULF WAR, 1990-1991

The Gulf War was Bush's greatest single foreign policy success. In 1990, Iraqi dictator **Saddam Hussein** invaded Kuwait, seizing its vast oil wealth and extending Iraq's bor-

ders. Hussein refused demands by the United Nations to withdraw. In response, U.N. forces under U.S. leadership attacked Iraq. The invasion quickly succeeded. In February 1991, all Iraqi troops were driven out of Kuwait, and Hussein agreed to pay Kuwait for damages. President Bush declared a cease-fire. The crisis was significant as the first major challenge to world order since the end of the Cold War. American influence was greatly enhanced by U.S. success in

U.S. soldiers fighting in the Gulf War

Jarrett Archives

the Gulf War. Bush used the upsurge in American prestige to bring about peace talks between Israel and its Arab neighbors in late 1991.

THE UNITED STATES TODAY

THE CLINTON PRESIDENCY, 1993-2001

Partly due to the recession, Bush lost the election of 1992 to **Bill Clinton**. Clinton promised **health care reform**, but could not get a plan through Congress. However, his economic policies and advances in computer technology were successful in restoring the economy. By the end of his Presidency, the economy was enjoying its best period in history — employment and business profits were at all-time highs, and the government had a series of budget surpluses.

SCANDAL AND IMPEACHMENT

Clinton became the subject of a scandal when an independent prosecutor learned of a sexual liaison between the President and a White House intern. After finding Clinton had lied about the relationship under oath, the prosecutor recommended **impeachment**. The House voted along party lines to impeach (*indict*) the President, but the Senate vote fell short of the two-thirds required to convict him.

FOREIGN POLICY

Clinton pushed the North American Free Trade Agreement (**NAFTA**) through Congress. First proposed during the Bush Administration, it created a trade association between the U.S., Canada and Mexico. When Serb nationalists persecuted Muslims in Kosovo, Clinton spearheaded the use of NATO forces to bomb Serbia, and ended the bloodshed. Clinton was a tireless negotiator in the peace talks between Israel and the Palestinians. He tried using economic threats against China to force them to improve their human rights, but he abandoned this approach when it met with little success.

THE GEORGE W. BUSH PRESIDENCY

George W. Bush, son of former President George H.W. Bush, was elected in 2000 in the closest Presidential election in U.S. history. Bush's opponent, Clinton's Vice President **Al Gore**, won the popular vote. However, in some states the margin was so narrow that the winner of the Electoral College was unclear. Gore challenged the Florida vote count, but the U.S. Supreme Court stopped a recount, making Bush the winner.

DOMESTIC POLICY

As President, Bush pushed through tax cuts to stimulate a lagging economy. He also introduced the **No Child Left Behind Act**, requiring states to test students in both English and mathematics.

THE WAR ON TERRORISM

On **September 11, 2001, al-Qaeda** terrorists hijacked U.S. airliners and crashed them into the Pentagon and the **World Trade Center**. Almost three thousand people were killed. President Bush declared a "War on Terrorism." Federal agents replaced private security at U.S. airports, and the **Office of Homeland Security** was created. When the Taliban government of Afghanistan refused to hand over **Osama bin Laden**, the U.S. invaded. This action led to the overthrow of the Taliban.

THE WAR IN IRAQ

Bush and other world leaders also insisted that **Saddam Hussein** prove that Iraq had no weapons of mass destruction (**WMD**). Iraq repeatedly denied it had such weapons. France, Germany, and Russia recommended U.N. inspectors be given more time to search for them. However, in 2003, President Bush gave Hussein 48 hours to resign and leave Iraq. When Hussein rejected this proposal, the U.S., Great Britain, and their allies attacked. U.S. forces entered Baghdad in early April, as Hussein's regime collapsed. Hussein was captured in 2003. After a trial, he was found guilty of war crimes and executed. Despite these successes, there were frequent attacks on coalition forces. Religious and ethnic rivalries continue to divide the Iraqi people.

THE 2004 PRESIDENTIAL ELECTION

In 2004, President Bush ran for a second term against Senator **John Kerry**. Bush won a second term as President defeating Kerry in another closely contested election.

THE "SURGE" IN IRAQ

By the end of 2006, a thousand people were being killed in Iraq each month. President Bush announced a new "surge" in 2007. Thousands of U.S. troops were added to secure local neighborhoods, guard Iraq's borders, and strike at al-Qaeda. This step reduced violence in Iraq, but Iraqi legislators demanded that U.S. forces withdraw.

HURRICANE KATRINA

Hurricane Katrina led to the flooding of New Orleans and other parts of the Gulf Coast. When the levees failed, more than 1,800 people lost their lives. Critics blamed President Bush for a slow response to the worst hurricane to strike the United States.

PRESIDENTIAL POWER IN THE AGE OF TERROR

Following the September 11, 2001 attacks, Congress passed the **USA Patriot Act**, giving the President special powers to combat terrorism. The Bush administration authorized the National Security Agency to wiretap suspect callers without obtaining a warrant. These "warrantless" wiretaps were later held to be unconstitutional.

To protect against terrorism, the Bush administration permitted "enhanced interrogation" on prisoners of war in Iraqi detention centers, especially at **Abu Ghraib** in Iraq. In 2006, the Supreme Court held that torture could not be used.

THE LEGACY OF PRESIDENT BUSH

President Bush's two terms have become known for his keeping the nation safe from further terrorist attacks. His critics point to the economic downturn at the end of his Presidency, the collapse of the banking system and the mortgage crisis.

THE BARACK OBAMA PRESIDENCY, 2009-2016

The 2008 Presidential campaign saw a young Senator from Illinois, **Barack Obama**, emerge as the Democratic nominee. The Republicans nominated Senator **John McCain**. Obama criticized the war in Iraq and the state of the U.S. economy. A severe financial crisis in the months just before the election helped Obama to become the first African-American to be elected President.

THE FINANCIAL CRISIS OF 2008-2009

In 2000, the stock market dropped in value, leading the Federal Reserve to lower interest rates to stimulate the economy. These lower interest rates sparked new home buying. Some banks began lending money to borrowers who could not afford homes. President Bush also pushed through a series of tax cuts. Overbuilding led housing prices to fall. When interest rates started to rise again, many homeowners could no longer afford to pay their mortgages, leading to a rise in home foreclosures. Soon the economy began to spin out of control and all available credit dried up. The Bush Administration sought to bail out several large companies and banks. Congress approved a $700 billion bailout package.

❖ **Obama Acts to Stem the Crisis.** Once in office, President Obama sought to stimulate the economy by creating jobs and rebuilding roads, schools, and bridges. In February 2009, Congress passed President Obama's **American Recovery and Reinvestment Act** to jumpstart the economy. Another $787 billion was to be spent in a bailout package to create new jobs, save existing ones, spur economic activity, and invest in long-term infrastructure. There was a separate bail-out for the auto industry, helping to save both Chrysler and General Motors. In July 2012, Obama signed the "Dodd-Frank Reform Act" to increase government oversight of banks and the sale of various financial products.

THE AFFORDABLE CARE ACT: "OBAMACARE"

President Obama focused on the passage of the **Affordable Care Act**, also known as "**Obamacare**," to provide health insurance to all Americans, while reducing health care costs. Passed in 2010, the law sets up health care exchanges where insurance can be purchased, and requires citizens to buy insurance or pay a penalty. Taxes are being raised on high money earners to help fund the benefits. The act was challenged but was upheld by the U.S. Supreme Court in 2012.

THE TEA PARTY AND THE DEBT CEILING

The passage of the stimulus package and health care reform led to a reaction against government spending, known as the "**Tea Party**," which helped Republicans gain control of the House of Representatives in 2010. Tea Party Republicans opposed raising the "debt ceiling" — the limit on how much the U.S. can borrow. This led to a drop in the nation's credit rating and began a debate on the national debt.

PRESIDENTIAL ELECTION OF 2012

Former Massachusetts Governor **Mitt Romney** won the Republican nomination in the 2012 election. Romney outperformed Obama in the first Presidential debate, but Obama did better in later debates and ultimately won re-election.

GUN CONTROL

In 2012, a mentally disturbed twenty-year old in Newtown, Connecticut, shot and killed twenty children and six adults, sparking a new debate on gun control. Obama proposed several gun control bills to Congress, but fear of government interference to the Second Amendment prevented any national legislation from being enacted.

FOREIGN TROUBLES CLOUD THE HORIZON

A term sometimes used to describe President Obama's foreign policy is the "**Obama Doctrine**," because he has tended to emphasize negotiation and cooperation instead of unilateralism in world affairs. President Obama seeks to make American foreign policy less focused on U.S. interests alone, and prefers to give greater consideration to the impact our actions may have on the attitudes of other nations towards us.

❖ **North Korea.** Despite its failing economy, North Korea has a large army and continues to be a global security threat. Following the death of his father in 2011, **Kim Jong-un** became Korea's supreme leader. Kim reestablished his grandfather's belligerent style and threatened the U.S. with a "pre-emptive nuclear attack." Obama has been trying to work with the Chinese and the United Nations to isolate North Korea.

❖ **Iran.** Iran continues to refine its nuclear ores, claiming it is developing a new source of energy for peacetime domestic purposes. Critics fear Iran is developing nuclear weapons, which will tip the regional balance of power in the Middle East. Iran also sponsors terrorist groups. President Obama has been criticized for failing to encourage anti-government demonstrators in Iran in 2009, fearing he might jeopardize peaceful diplomacy to limit Iran's nuclear program.

❖ **Afghanistan.** Early in his Presidency, President Obama increased troop levels in Afghanistan. He also began devoting greater resources to revitalize Afghanistan's economic development, while pressing the government to reduce corruption and end the opium trade. Obama's Afghan policy focused on defeating al-Qaeda. He began to withdraw U.S. forces from Afghanistan in 2011. Obama hopes to have U.S. troops out by the summer of 2014.

❖ **Iraq.** Despite continued violence in Iraq, President Obama sought to end direct U.S. military involvement. He ended U.S. combat operations there in August 2010 and withdrew U.S. forces by the end of 2011.

❖ **Pakistan.** Obama enjoyed some of his greatest successes in Pakistan, where he expanded U.S. Predator strikes against terrorists in hiding and ordered the secret U.S. Navy Seal raid that killed Osama bin Laden.

❖ **China.** Despite President Obama's diplomatic overtures to the Chinese, they have resisted demands to enforce intellectual property rights, to weaken their currency, and to halt the stealing of U.S. technology through cyber-espionage.

❖ **Israeli-Palestinian Conflict.** President Obama has sought to work with both Israelis and Palestinians to achieve a two-state solution: a Jewish state in Israel and an Arab state in Palestine, living side-by-side in peace. In a speech in Jerusalem in 2013, Obama recognized that Israel has had to face Palestinian acts of terror, but argued strongly for recognizing Palestinians' right to self-determination and justice.

PRESIDENT OBAMA AND THE ARAB SPRING

In 2010, a dispute between a street peddler and a Tunisian policewoman led the peddler to set himself on fire in protest. Demonstrations against the Tunisian government broke out and soon spread from Tunisia to the rest of North Africa and the Middle East.

- **Egypt**. In Egypt, long-time pro-Western dictator Hosni Mubarak was overthrown. Mubarak was succeeded by **Mohammed Morsi**, Egypt's first democratically elected president. Morsi was a member of the Muslim Brotherhood, a group of Islamic Fundamentalists. Despite increasing disorder and a government less friendly to the United States, President Obama remains committed to democracy in Egypt.

- **Libya**. In Libya, President Obama refrained from taking military action, but supported air strikes and intervention of NATO forces. Eventually, dictator **Colonel Gaddafi** was overthrown and killed. Obama was criticized for the slow State Department response to terrorist attacks on the U.S. Consulate in Benghazi, which led to the murders of the U.S. Ambassador and three other Americans.

- **Syria**. When a civil war began in Syria against dictator **Bashar al-Assad**, President Obama refused to enter the conflict. Faced with the slaughter of thousands of Syrians, Obama faced mounting pressure to adopt a "no-fly" zone over Syria. He warned that Syria's use of chemical weapons against its people might bring U.S. action.

President Obama's greatest foreign policy accomplishments were the killing of Osama bin Laden, the withdrawal of U.S. forces from Iraq and Afghanistan, and the use of "drone" attacks against the leadership of al-Qaeda. During Obama's second term, he faces greater competition from China, growing threats from Iran and North Korea, and continued instability in the Middle East.

TOWARD A POST-INDUSTRIAL WORLD

Just as important as recent government policies have been several long-term developments that have altered the American way of life.

TECHNOLOGY

The U.S. began as an agricultural nation, then evolved to an industrial powerhouse. In the last fifty years, the nation has shifted from an industrial economy to a "post-industrial" or service economy. Americans are now more likely to work as salespeople, computer programmers, bank tellers or teachers than as factory workers. Much of the increased productivity of the economy was due to computers. The **Internet**, a world-wide linking of computers, makes it easier to communicate and find information.

ENERGY

Population growth and rising living standards have increased energy demands. Nuclear power was expected to provide energy without pollution, but an accident at **Three Mile Island** in 1979 showed it could be unsafe. New oil sources in Alaska and the oceans have helped meet our energy needs, while Americans continue to emphasize conservation and the development of new energy sources such as solar, wind and hydro (*water*) power.

THE ENVIRONMENT

As more countries develop and the world's population grows, pollution of the earth's air, water and other resources poses an ever-increasing threat to human survival.

❖ **Global Warming**. Some pollutants in the atmosphere prevent heat from escaping into space. This **greenhouse effect** may permanently raise temperatures enough to cause farmland to become desert, or polar ices to melt, raising ocean levels.

❖ **Acid Rain**. When coal and oil are burned, they emit pollutants into the atmosphere. Many pollutants released by industry and automobile exhaust turn into acids, which get washed out of the air when it rains. When these pollutants return to the ground, they are highly toxic — killing fish and destroying forests.

❖ **Thinning of the Ozone Layer**. The ozone layer absorbs dangerous ultraviolet radiation from the sun, which would otherwise cause skin cancer and other diseases. However, the ozone layer has been rapidly eroded by widespread fluorocarbon use.

❖ **Water Pollution**. As cities become more crowded, their ability to handle increased sewage and waste is strained. Often this leads to the dumping of raw sewage into nearby lakes and rivers, contaminating drinking water.

A CHANGING POPULATION

Americans face new challenges from a changing population. The south and west are attracting increasing numbers of people, straining existing water and power supplies. America is becoming more diverse, especially with the growth of the Hispanic population and rising levels of immigration. Americans are also living longer. Medical advances have increased the number of people who live into their 70s and 80s. As the **"baby boomers"** (those born between 1945 and 1965) begin to retire, there is concern that the Social Security system will not have enough money to fund their retirements.

CHECKING YOUR UNDERSTANDING

KEY TERMS AND CONCEPTS

- ✦ Détente
- ✦ Watergate Scandal
- ✦ Panama Canal Treaty
- ✦ Camp David Accords
- ✦ "Reaganomics"
- ✦ New Federalism
- ✦ Iran-Contra Affair
- ✦ Gulf War of 1990
- ✦ Global Warming

MULTIPLE-CHOICE QUESTIONS

1   The resolution of the Watergate scandal reinforced the idea that
   1   our government is based on the rule of laws, not individuals
   2   our chief executive has unlimited powers
   3   Congress is not effective in dealing with a constitutional crisis
   4   the Supreme Court cannot make decisions affecting the Presidency

2   During the administration of President Nixon, U.S. policy toward China was characterized by
   1   repeated attempts to introduce democracy into China
   2   increasing hostility and isolation
   3   the signing of a mutual defense pact
   4   a relaxation of strained relations

3   Which best explains why Presidential power increased during the Vietnam War?
   1   Congress ignored the war in favor of domestic issues.
   2   The Constitution was suspended during wartime.
   3   The President was in the best position to act quickly and decisively.
   4   In wartime, the Constitution puts all power into the President's hands.

4   The Camp David Accords, negotiated by President Carter, were significant because they represented
   1   the first major peace agreement between Israel and an Arab nation
   2   the establishment of a worldwide human rights policy
   3   a lasting arms-reduction treaty
   4   the end of the Vietnam War

5   During President Reagan's two terms in office, his federal budget proposals came under sharp criticism because they
   1   lowered interest rates
   2   increased social welfare spending
   3   advocated raising the income tax
   4   included very large deficits

6 Which statement best reflects President Nixon's "New Federalism"?
1 The federal government should be given greater power.
2 Taxes should be raised to reduce the federal deficit.
3 The federal government should give power back to the states.
4 Military spending should be cut to provide funds for social programs.

7 President Wilson's Fourteen Points and President Carter's Camp David Accords are examples of U.S. actions aimed at promoting
1 international trade
2 world peace
3 improved environmental standards
4 effective communication networks

8 Which event took place during the administration of President George Bush?
1 invasion of Panama
2 passage of the Civil Rights Act
3 passage of the New Deal
4 the Watergate scandal

9 One direct result of the Persian Gulf War was that the United States
1 gained control of oil resources in the Middle East
2 liberated Kuwait from Iraqi control
3 was able to promote peace between Israel and its Arab neighbors
4 seized colonies in the Middle East

THEMATIC ESSAY QUESTION

Directions: Write a well-organized essay that includes an introduction, several paragraphs addressing the task below, and a conclusion.

Theme: Justice and Human Rights

> Throughout our history, members of certain groups in American society have faced prejudice or discrimination.

Task:

> Choose **two** groups from your study of American history.
> For *each* group:
> • *Discuss* some prejudice or discrimination faced by members of that group.
> • *Describe* how the group overcame that prejudice or discrimination.

You may use any examples from your study American history. Some suggestions you might wish to consider include: Native American Indians, African Americans, women, Irish Americans, new immigrants, Japanese Americans, Jewish Americans, Hispanic Americans, and Americans with disabilities.

You are *not* limited to these suggestions.

CHAPTER 12

A FINAL REVIEW

This chapter provides several approaches for a final review of the information that appears most frequently in questions on the U.S. History and Government Regents Examination, including a list of notable Americans, a checklist of important terms, and two charts showing milestones of U.S. domestic history and foreign policy.

FORTY-FOUR NOTABLE AMERICANS

Following is a checklist of individuals who are frequently the focus of multiple-choice and thematic essay questions, and the page where they can be found.

- ❑ Anthony, Susan B. (67)
- ❑ Bush, George (120)
- ❑ Carnegie, Andrew (53)
- ❑ Carter, Jimmy (117)
- ❑ Douglass, Frederick (39)
- ❑ DuBois, W.E.B (43)
- ❑ Edison, Thomas (52)
- ❑ Ford, Gerald (117)
- ❑ Ford, Henry (81)
- ❑ Friedan, Betty (110)
- ❑ Gompers, Samuel (55)
- ❑ Hamilton, Alexander (36)
- ❑ Hoover, Herbert (85)
- ❑ Jackson, Andrew (37)
- ❑ Jackson, Helen Hunt (59)
- ❑ Jefferson, Thomas (22)
- ❑ Johnson, Andrew (41)
- ❑ Johnson, Lyndon B. (108)
- ❑ Kennedy, John F. (108)
- ❑ King, Martin Luther, Jr. (106)
- ❑ Lincoln, Abraham (40)
- ❑ Malcolm X (111)
- ❑ Marshall, John (30)
- ❑ McCarthy, Joseph (98)
- ❑ McKinley, William (68)
- ❑ Nixon, Richard (116)
- ❑ Paine, Thomas (22)
- ❑ Parks, Rosa (106)
- ❑ Perry, Matthew (70)
- ❑ Reagan, Ronald (118)
- ❑ Robinson, Jackie (105)
- ❑ Rockefeller, John D. (53)
- ❑ Roosevelt, Franklin D. (85)
- ❑ Roosevelt, Theodore (66)
- ❑ Scott, Dred (39)
- ❑ Sinclair, Upton (65)
- ❑ Stanton, Elizabeth Cady (67)
- ❑ Stowe, Harriet Beecher (39)
- ❑ Truman, Harry S (97)
- ❑ Tubman, Harriet (39)
- ❑ Warren, Earl (105)
- ❑ Washington, Booker T. (43)
- ❑ Washington, George (36)
- ❑ Wilson, Woodrow (71)

CHECKLIST OF IMPORTANT TERMS AND CONCEPTS

This checklist of terms and concepts also includes those events, organizations, and Supreme Court cases *(and the page numbers where they are found)* that are frequently the focus of multiple-choice, thematic, and document-based essay questions.

- ❒ Affirmative Action (107)
- ❒ American Revolution (22)
- ❒ Articles of Confederation (23)
- ❒ Bill of Rights (31)
- ❒ *Brown v. Board of Education* (105)
- ❒ Camp David Accords (118)
- ❒ Checks and Balances (27)
- ❒ Civil War (39)
- ❒ Civil Rights Movement (105)
- ❒ Cold War (95)
- ❒ Cuban Missile Crisis (108)
- ❒ Dawes Act (59)
- ❒ Declaration of Independence (22)
- ❒ Elastic Clause (27)
- ❒ Electoral College (29)
- ❒ Emancipation Proclamation (40)
- ❒ *Federalist Papers* (25)
- ❒ Fourteen Points (72)
- ❒ Fourteenth Amendment (41)
- ❒ Grange Movement (63)
- ❒ Great Compromise (24)
- ❒ Great Depression (83)
- ❒ Harlem Renaissance (83)
- ❒ Homestead Act (59)
- ❒ Industrial Revolution (52
- ❒ Isolationism (91)
- ❒ Jacksonian Democracy (37)
- ❒ "Jim Crow" Laws (43)
- ❒ Judicial Review (30)
- ❒ Korean War (97)
- ❒ League of Nations (72)
- ❒ Louisiana Purchase (36)
- ❒ Manifest Destiny (38)
- ❒ Marshall Plan (96)
- ❒ *Marbury v. Madison* (30)

- ❒ Mercantilism (21)
- ❒ Mexican-American War (38)
- ❒ Monroe Doctrine (37)
- ❒ Muckrakers (65)
- ❒ Nativism (80)
- ❒ NATO (96)
- ❒ New Deal (85)
- ❒ New Immigrants (57)
- ❒ Nineteenth Amendment (67)
- ❒ Open Door Policy (69)
- ❒ *Plessy v. Ferguson* (43)
- ❒ Popular Sovereignty (26)
- ❒ Populism (63)
- ❒ Progressive Movement (65)
- ❒ Prohibition (82)
- ❒ Reconstruction Era (41)
- ❒ Red Scare (80)
- ❒ *Roe v. Wade* (110)
- ❒ Sectionalism (39)
- ❒ Seneca Falls Convention (67)
- ❒ Separation of Powers (26)
- ❒ Sherman Anti-Trust Act (54)
- ❒ Social Security Act (87)
- ❒ Spanish-American War (68)
- ❒ Third Parties (64)
- ❒ Truman Doctrine (96)
- ❒ Unwritten Constitution (28)
- ❒ Urbanization (56)
- ❒ Vietnam War (112)
- ❒ War Powers Act (112)
- ❒ War of 1812 (37)
- ❒ Watergate Scandal (116)
- ❒ Women's Rights Movement (67)
- ❒ World War I (71)
- ❒ World War II (92)

MILESTONES OF UNITED STATES DOMESTIC HISTORY

MILESTONE	DESCRIPTION
The American Revolution (1775-1783)	Colonists became alarmed when the British imposed new taxes without their consent. On July 4, 1776, members of the Continental Congress issued the Declaration of Independence, proclaiming that the purpose of government is to protect the rights of the governed. The American Revolutionary War began.
The Constitutional Convention and Bill of Rights (1787-1791)	After independence, the Articles of Confederation created a central government which could not defend against rebellion or invasion, or prohibit states from taxing one another's goods. States sent delegates to Philadelphia to write a new Constitution with a national President, Congress, and Supreme Court. The states ratified it in 1788. A Bill of Rights was added in 1791.
Creation of the National Economy	The Commerce Clause of the Constitution and the Supreme Court decision in *Gibbons v. Ogden* (1824) helped create a national economy in which citizens could do business in other states on equal terms — encouraging the free movement of goods, money and people. This greatly speeded the growth of the U.S. economy.
Industrial Revolution	Factories, and the use of new machines and sources of power greatly increased the scale of production, changed where people lived, and altered what they produced and consumed.
Westward Expansion (1803-1848)	After the American Revolution, settlers streamed across the Appalachians to settle the Northwest Territory. The Louisiana Purchase doubled the size of the nation. Americans next annexed California and the Southwest after their victory in the Mexican-American War — giving them territory from the Atlantic to the Pacific Ocean.
The Civil War (1861-1865)	Sectionalism grew as different ways of life emerged. Southerners relied on slavery, as abolitionism grew stronger in the North. The acquisition of new territories created a crisis as Americans debated whether to extend slavery to these areas. When Lincoln was elected in 1860, Southern states seceded. Seeking to preserve the Union, Lincoln led the nation into the Civil War. The North finally achieved victory in 1865, after four years of war.

MILESTONE	DESCRIPTION
Reconstruction (1865-1877)	During Reconstruction, Americans had to reunify the nation and rebuild the South. Radical Republicans in Congress refused to recognize Southern state governments and imposed military rule. Reconstruction ended in 1877 when Northern troops were withdrawn. White Southerners then deprived African Americans of their voting rights and introduced racial segregation.
Industrialization and the Settlement of the West	After the Civil War, America was transformed by industrialization, urbanization, immigration, the expansion of the railroads, and the settlement of the Great Plains and Far West. Native American Indians were forced onto reservations.
Urbanization and Immigration (late 1880s)	A new urban culture developed as the nation was transformed into a nation of city-dwellers. Cities became crowded and faced housing shortages. As need for labor grew, immigrants filled jobs in factories and sweatshops. Despite facing many hardships, they contributed greatly to the creation of a prosperous economy.
Grangers and Populists (1867-1896)	High railroad charges and falling food prices led farmers to organize into Grange associations. Later, farmers joined the Populist Party, which sought many reforms including party primaries and a graduated income tax, later adopted by other political parties.
Progressive Era (1900-1920)	Muckrakers and other middle-class reformers exposed the abuses caused by the rise of big business and rapid industrialization. Progressive state governments and Presidents Theodore Roosevelt and Woodrow Wilson helped curb some of the worst abuses.
Establishment of the Federal Reserve and the Income Tax (1912-1913)	President Wilson introduced a Federal Reserve System to provide stability and flexibility to our national monetary system, and a progressive income tax to raise revenue. The Federal Reserve helped stabilize the economy, while income taxes became the main source of federal revenue, replacing tariffs.
Mass Production of the Automobile	The rise of automobiles created a new industry employing millions of Americans. Cars, buses and trucks increased personal mobility, brought different parts of the country closer together, and transformed the American way of life.
Roaring Twenties (1920s)	The passage of the 19th Amendment and the prosperity of the 1920s saw the rise of new cultural values. Women, African Americans, and youths enjoyed more freedom than ever before.

MILESTONE	DESCRIPTION
Depression, the New Deal, and World War II (1930s-1940s)	The New York Stock Market Crash of 1929 led to the Great Depression. President Roosevelt's "New Deal," experimented with new programs to find people work and introduced Social Security and many other reforms. World War II restored full employment as the nation fought against Germany and Japan.
Post-War Prosperity (1950s-1960s)	After World War II, America emerged as the world's leading economic superpower. Americans bought millions of autos, refrigerators, and other appliances. War veterans moved to suburbs and started families, creating the baby boom.
Civil Rights Movement (1950s-1960s)	The *Brown* decision (1954) and the Montgomery Bus Boycott (1955-56) started the Civil Rights Movement. Under Martin Luther King, Jr. and others, African Americans ended racial segregation and made tremendous strides towards racial equality.
The 1960s: A Decade of Change	The Civil Rights Movement was followed by the Women's Liberation Movement, in which women achieved greater equality in the workplace and the home. President Johnson attempted to eliminate poverty with his "Great Society" Programs. A new youth culture emerged in which young people experimented with sexual freedom, new fashions and music, and drugs. The war in Vietnam led to the disillusionment of many with the so-called "Establishment."
The Presidency in Crisis (1968-1979)	The New Deal, World War II, Cold War, and Vietnam War led to tremendous increases in Presidential power. The failure in Vietnam and President Nixon's resignation over the Watergate scandal led to widespread doubts about the capabilities of our nation's leaders. Presidents Ford and Carter had difficulties coping with rising oil prices, stagflation, and foreign crises.
America Today (1980-Present)	Under Presidents Reagan, Bush, and Clinton, Americans enjoyed a return to prosperity, followed by recession, and then the largest period of economic expansion the nation has ever seen. The Reagan and Bush Presidencies witnessed the end of the Cold War and the collapse of the Soviet Union. Under Clinton, Americans benefited from increased foreign trade and from advances in computers and other technologies.

MILESTONES OF AMERICAN FOREIGN POLICY

MILESTONE	DESCRIPTION
Washington's Farewell Address (1896)	President Washington advised Americans to avoid entangling alliances with European nations. This policy helped the United States keep out of war between France and England until 1812.
War of 1812	In 1812, Congress declared war against the British to stop the impressment of U.S. sailors and to try, unsuccessfully, to conquer Canada. The war ended in December 1814, with little changed.
Monroe Doctrine (1823)	President Monroe announced U.S. opposition to any European attempt to reconquer former colonies in the Western Hemisphere that were independent, or to establish new colonies. As a result, the newly independent nations of Latin America kept their independence.
Manifest Destiny (mid-1800s)	Many Americans believed the U.S. was fated to expand from the Atlantic to the Pacific. The desire for expansion led to the Mexican-American War (1846-1848). Mexico was defeated and forced to surrender much of its territory to the United States.
Spanish-American War (1898)	After the DeLôme letter and sinking of the U.S.S. *Maine*, America warred with Spain to help Cuban rebels win independence. After the Americans won the war, Cuba fell under U.S. control. Spain lost the Philippines and its possessions in the Western hemisphere.
American Imperialism (1898-1900)	After the Spanish-American War, the nation became an imperialist power, annexing the Philippines, Puerto Rico, Hawaii, and Samoa. Americans also developed trade with China and Japan.
Panama Canal and the Big Stick Policy (1902-1914)	Theodore Roosevelt reached an agreement with newly independent Panama for construction of the Panama Canal. Roosevelt used his "Big Stick" Policy to assert a greater U.S. presence in the Caribbean. The Caribbean Sea became an "American lake" under the control and domination of the United States.
World War I (1917-1918)	Events in Europe led to war in 1914. America was neutral, but entered the war in 1917 after German submarines attacked American ships. American entry led to an Allied victory by 1918. Germany surrendered and a revolution in Germany turned that country into a democracy.
The Fourteen Points and the Treaty of Versailles (1918-1919)	President Wilson announced America's war aims in the Fourteen Points, including the creation of a League of Nations — an international peace organization. Many of Wilson's ideas were accepted in the Treaty of Versailles but the U.S. Senate, fearing another war, rejected the treaty and the League of Nations. The U.S. became isolationist.

MILESTONE	DESCRIPTION
World War II **(1939-1945)**	World War II broke out when Germany invaded Poland. At first, America was neutral. In 1941, Germany's ally, Japan, attacked the U.S. fleet at Pearl Harbor, bringing the U.S. into the war. World War II was the most destructive war in history. It ended in 1945, after Americans dropped atomic bombs on two Japanese cities.
The Cold War **(1946-1989)**	After World War II, America and the Soviet Union emerged as superpowers. When the Soviets established Communist governments in Eastern Europe, the "Cold War" began. Germany was divided in two, and an Iron Curtain fell between Eastern and Western Europe. The Western allies formed NATO, and the Soviet Union and its satellites formed the Warsaw Pact. Although both Superpowers never went to war with each other, they stockpiled nuclear weapons and missiles and became involved in numerous regional crises.
Korean War **(1950-1953)**	In 1950, Communist North Korea invaded South Korea. Acting under a United Nations resolution, President Truman sent troops to South Korea to repel the North Korean attack. When U.S. forces advanced into North Korea, Communist China entered the war on the side of North Korea. After three years of fighting, a truce was signed leaving Korea divided much as it was before the war.
Vietnam War **(1964-1973)**	After Vietnam won independence from France, Communist North Vietnam began a war against the non-Communist South to reunite the country under Communist rule. U.S. troops were sent to aid the South Vietnamese, but were unable to defeat the Viet Cong and North Vietnamese. America finally withdrew. Thousands of Americans were killed. In Vietnam, a million people were killed, and millions more were left homeless. Difficulties in Vietnam also led President Nixon to open relations with Communist China and to pursue détente with the Soviet Union.
The Persian Gulf War **(1990)**	Iraqi dictator Saddam Hussein invaded oil-rich Kuwait. President Bush, with U.N. support, launched an invasion of Kuwait and Iraq, forcing an Iraqi withdrawal. The Gulf War was the first example of multinational cooperation after the end of the Cold War. The allies were able to liberate Kuwait, but stopped short of toppling Saddam Hussein in Iraq.
Bosnia and Kosovo **(1990-1999)**	After the end of the Cold War, several ethnic groups in Yugoslavia declared their independence. After years of fighting, U.S. and NATO forces intervened and achieved a negotiated settlement. The pattern was repeated in Kosovo, where NATO air power was used to halt Serb attacks on civilians.

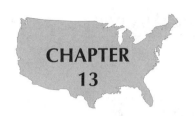

CHAPTER 13

A PRACTICE REGENTS EXAMINATION: January 2013

Now that you have reviewed the material in this book, you are ready to take a practice test to measure your progress. To help you in this assessment, this chapter has a complete practice U.S. History and Government Regents Examination. However, before you begin, let's look at some common-sense tips for taking such tests:

- ✦ **Answer All Questions**. Don't leave questions unanswered. Since there is **no** penalty for guessing, answer all questions — even if only making a guess

- ✦ **Use the Process of Elimination**. After reading a multiple-choice question, even if you don't know the right answer, it may be clear that certain choices are wrong. Some choices may be irrelevant because they relate to a different time or place. Other choices may have no connection with the question or may be inaccurate statements. After you have eliminated all the wrong choices, choose the best response that remains.

- ✦ **Read the Question Carefully**. Underline key words or expressions that are central to the question. If a word in the question is unfamiliar, break the word down into words that are familiar. Look at the prefix (*start of the word*), root, or suffix (*ending*) for clues to the meaning of the word.

Taking the examination that follows will help you to identify any areas that you still need to study. Good luck on this practice test!

U.S. HISTORY AND GOVERNMENT JANUARY 2013 REGENTS

This practice U.S. History and Government Regents Examination contains three parts:

Part I 50 multiple-choice questions	**Part II** one thematic essay	**Part III** one document-based essay

PART I: ANSWER ALL QUESTIONS IN THIS PART

1 Which geographic factor most directly influenced the location of the first English settlements in North America?
   (1) rivers along the Atlantic coast
   (2) availability of flat land in the Midwest
   (3) mild climate along the Gulf coast
   (4) forests throughout the Middle Colonies

2 The Magna Carta and the English Bill of Rights were significant influences on United States constitutional development because they
   (1) provided suffrage for all men and women
   (2) placed limits on the powers of the government
   (3) called for the abolition of slavery
   (4) supported the development of federalism

3 The Declaration of Independence contains a
   (1) proposal for reuniting the colonies and England
   (2) statement of grievances against the King of England
   (3) request for a treaty between the colonies and Spain
   (4) plan for organizing the western territories

4 Which set of events related to early America is in the correct chronological order?
   (1) inauguration of George Washington ! passage of Stamp Act !Battle of Saratoga ! French and Indian War
   (2) Battle of Saratoga !French and Indian War ! passage of Stamp Act ! inauguration of George Washington
   (3) French and Indian War ! passage of Stamp Act ! Battle of Saratoga ! inauguration of George Washington
   (4) passage of Stamp Act ! French and Indian War !inauguration of George Washington ! Battle of Saratoga

5 Critics of the Articles of Confederation argued that it
   (1) imposed unfair taxes on the states
   (2) used a draft to raise a national army
   (3) provided a strong system of federal courts
   (4) placed too much power in the hands of the states

6 "… Article 6. There shall be neither slavery nor involuntary servitude in the said territory, otherwise than in the punishment of crimes whereof the party shall have been duly convicted: Provided, always, That any person escaping into the same, from whom labor or service is lawfully claimed in any one of the original States, such fugitive may be lawfully reclaimed and conveyed to the person claiming his or her labor or service as aforesaid.…"
   — Northwest Ordinance, 1787

Based on this excerpt from the Northwest Ordinance, which statement is a valid conclusion?
   (1) The issue of slavery was largely ignored before the Civil War.
   (2) Abolitionists had gained control of the Constitutional Convention.
   (3) Slavery was legally banned in the Northwest Territory.
   (4) Enslaved persons had constitutionally protected civil rights.

7 The Great Compromise enabled delegates at the Constitutional Convention (1787) to
   (1) establish the principle of popular sovereignty in the territories
   (2) give Congress the exclusive right to declare war if the nation is attacked
   (3) protect the interests of states with small populations and states with large populations
   (4) provide for the indirect election of the president through the electoral college

8 Which presidential action is an example of the use of the unwritten constitution?
(1) signing a law passed by Congress
(2) calling a meeting of the cabinet
(3) ordering the navy to patrol the Persian Gulf
(4) nominating a federal court judge

9 The major benefit of having the elastic clause in the United States Constitution is that it
(1) allows the government to respond to changing conditions
(2) protects the rights of racial minorities
(3) prevents one branch of government from becoming too powerful
(4) establishes a postal service

10 How did Alexander Hamilton's financial plan affect the economy of the United States during the 1790s?
(1) National tax revenues decreased.
(2) High tariffs increased foreign trade.
(3) Treasury policies contributed to widespread inflation.
(4) The newly created Bank of the United States helped stabilize the economy.

11 One result of the purchase of the Louisiana Territory (1803) was that the United States
(1) acquired California from Spain
(2) gained control of the port of New Orleans
(3) ended border conflicts with British Canada
(4) annexed Florida

12 The decision in Marbury v. Madison (1803) was significant because it established that the Supreme Court
(1) had limited powers over state courts
(2) had the power to choose its own members
(3) could declare a federal law unconstitutional
(4) could impeach the president and other government officials

13 The constitutional controversy that led directly to the start of the Civil War concerned the right of states to
(1) control tariff rates
(2) sign treaties with foreign nations
(3) redraw congressional districts
(4) secede from the Union

14 Which group benefited most directly from the Supreme Court decision in Dred Scott v. Sanford (1857)?
(1) abolitionists
(2) immigrants
(3) slave owners
(4) enslaved persons

15 Which title best completes the partial outline below?

I. _____

   A. California Gold Rush (1849)
   B. Homestead Act (1862)
   C. Completion of transcontinental railroad (1869)

(1) Factors Encouraging Westward Settlement
(2) Government-Sponsored Transportation Programs
(3) Recognition of Native American Indian Land Rights
(4) Actions Promoting the Conservation of Natural Resources

Base your answer to question 16 on the passage from the trial transcript below and on your knowledge of social studies.

... MISS ANTHONY: When I was brought before your honor for trial, I hoped for a broad and liberal interpretation of the Constitution and its recent amendments, that should declare all United States citizens under its protecting aegis [shield]—that should declare equality of rights the national guarantee to all persons born or naturalized in the United States. But failing to get this justice—failing, even, to get a trial by a jury *not* of my peers—I ask not leniency at your hands—but rather the full rigors of the law....

Source: *United States* v. *Susan B. Anthony*, 1873

16 The constitutional amendments referred to in this statement were ratified to
(1) end the importation of slaves
(2) increase federal revenue
(3) institute national Prohibition
(4) provide legal rights to African Americans

17 Which statement best describes how the status of African Americans in the South changed soon after the end of Reconstruction in 1877?
(1) The Supreme Court consistently supported civil rights for African Americans.
(2) Poll taxes and literacy tests were eliminated for African Americans.
(3) Increasing numbers of African Americans were elected to public office.
(4) African Americans faced increasing discrimination and segregation.

18 The theory of laissez-faire economics was used during the late 1800s to
(1) justify unregulated business growth
(2) call for more consumer protection
(3) support Progressive programs
(4) achieve equal distribution of income

Base your answers to questions 19 and 20 on the speakers' statements below and on your knowledge of social studies.

Speaker A: The best way to prevent corruption in government is to allow citizens a direct role in the legislative process.
Speaker B: Breaking up trusts and monopolies will increase business competition.
Speaker C: An important goal of the federal government should be the protection of our natural resources.
Speaker D: Government will only improve when women are granted full suffrage.

19 Which speaker's statement is most directly related to the political concepts of initiative, referendum, and recall?
(1) A   (3) C
(2) B   (4) D

20 Which two speakers' viewpoints reflect actions taken by Theodore Roosevelt when he was president (1901–1909)?
(1) A and B   (3) C and D
(2) B and C   (4) D and A

21 The term *muckraker* was used in the early 1900s to describe writers who
(1) supported limits on government regulation
(2) exposed abuses in American society
(3) wanted the United States to ban all immigration
(4) promoted racial integration efforts

22 In the early 1900s, the United States proposed the Open Door policy to
(1) gain new colonies in the Pacific
(2) win support for building the Panama Canal
(3) improve relations with Europe
(4) secure access to markets in China

23 Which title best completes the partial outline below?

I. _____

   A. No government without consent of the governed

   B. High cost of defending territories outside the United States

   C. United States tradition of noninvolvement

(1) America's New Immigration Policy
(2) Reasons for Overseas Expansion
(3) Causes of the Spanish-American War
(4) Arguments Opposing Imperialism

24 The Federal Reserve System was created in 1913 to
(1) authorize Congress to set interest rates
(2) regulate the nation's money supply
(3) allow the government to own the nation's banks
(4) take over the responsibility of printing money

Base your answers to questions 25 and 26 on the map below and on your knowledge of social studies.

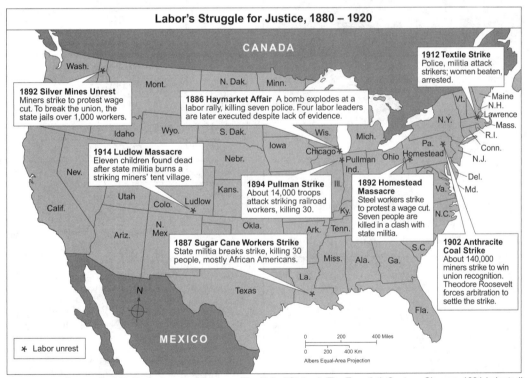

Source: Gary B. Nash, American Odyssey: The United States in The Twentieth Century, Glencoe, 1994 (adapted)

25 Which generalization about labor unions in the United States is most clearly supported by information on the map?
(1) The federal government supported labor union activities.
(2) Strikes by labor unions were often suppressed by government actions.
(3) Labor union membership was limited to mine workers.
(4) State governments offered to arbitrate labor disputes.

26 Which was the first labor strike to end with the president intervening on behalf of the workers?
(1) 1886 Haymarket Affair
(2) 1894 Pullman Strike
(3) 1902 Anthracite Coal Strike
(4) 1912 Textile Strike

Base your answer to question 27 on the posters below and on your knowledge of social studies.

Source: Library of Congress

27 The United States government published these World War I posters to encourage Americans to
(1) increase military enlistments
(2) reduce the use of consumer goods
(3) invest in the war effort
(4) conserve scarce resources for the military

28 After World War I, one way in which the Red Scare, the passing of the Quota Acts, and the growth of the Ku Klux Klan were similar is that they all
(1) exploited fears about people who were considered un-American
(2) encouraged the assimilation of new immigrants into American society
(3) supported the goals of the suffrage movement
(4) exhibited prejudice against African Americans

Base your answer to question 29 on the chart below and on your knowledge of social studies.

Depression Era Unemployment Statistics

Year	Number of Unemployed	Percentage of Civilian Labor Force
1929	1,550,000	3.2
1930	4,340,000	8.9
1931	8,020,000	16.3
1932	12,060,000	24.1
1933	12,830,000	25.2
1934	11,340,000	22.0
1935	10,610,000	20.3
1936	9,030,000	17.0
1937	7,700,000	14.3
1938	10,390,000	19.1
1939	9,480,000	17.2
1940	8,120,000	14.6
1941	5,560,000	9.9
1942	2,660,000	4.7
1943	1,070,000	1.9
1944	670,000	1.2
1945	1,040,000	1.9

Source: U.S. Bureau of the Census

29 Which conclusion is most clearly supported by the information in the chart?
(1) President Herbert Hoover's economic policies expanded job opportunities.
(2) The United States unemployment rate reached its highest level in 1938.
(3) President Franklin D. Roosevelt's New Deal programs failed to address the unemployment crisis.
(4) World War II ended the high unemployment rates of the Great Depression.

30 As part of the New Deal, the Securities and Exchange Commission (SEC) and the Federal Deposit Insurance Corporation (FDIC) were created to
 (1) allow for a quick recovery of stock prices
 (2) provide direct loans to businesses
 (3) protect individual investors from stock fraud and bank failure
 (4) allow banks and companies to invest in the stock market

31 Senator Huey Long, Dr. Francis Townsend, and Father Charles Coughlin are best known as
 (1) members of President Franklin D. Roosevelt's cabinet
 (2) outspoken critics of President Franklin D. Roosevelt's New Deal
 (3) supporters of President Franklin D. Roosevelt's reelection campaign in 1940
 (4) members of the Supreme Court nominated by President Franklin D. Roosevelt

32 The "cash and carry" policy and the Lend-Lease Act were used by the United States to
 (1) help fund League of Nations efforts to maintain peace
 (2) encourage British appeasement of Germany
 (3) fulfill treaty obligations with Great Britain and France
 (4) provide support for the Allies in World War II without entering the war

33 President Franklin D. Roosevelt referred to December 7, 1941, as "a date which will live in infamy" because on that day
 (1) Germany invaded Poland
 (2) Japan attacked Pearl Harbor
 (3) Italy declared war on the United States
 (4) the United States dropped an atomic bomb on Hiroshima

Base your answer to question 34 on the postcard below and on your knowledge of social studies.

Source: The Authentic History Center (adapted)

34 Which constitutional amendment was adopted in response to the issue raised on this postcard?
 (1) graduated income tax
 (2) direct election of United States senators
 (3) ban on poll taxes in presidential elections
 (4) limit on the number of years a president can serve

35 In *Korematsu v. United States* (1944), the Supreme Court upheld the military order excluding Japanese Americans from the West Coast on the basis that the action was considered
 (1) a matter of national security
 (2) a necessity for the economy
 (3) an attempt to limit immigration from Japan
 (4) a way to protect Japanese Americans from anti-Japanese hysteria

Base your answers to questions 36 and 37 on the cartoon below and on your knowledge of social studies.

"He's finally getting the hang of it."

Source: Dorman Smith, Phoenix Gazette, 1949 (adapted)

36 Which statement most accurately expresses the main idea of the cartoon?
  (1) American taxpayers hope the Marshall Plan will quickly stabilize Europe's economy.
  (2) The Marshall Plan will limit Europe's economic recovery.
  (3) Europe will not take advantage of the Marshall Plan.
  (4) The Marshall Plan will bankrupt the American taxpayer.

37 The United States undertook the action shown in the cartoon primarily to
  (1) keep the Soviet Union from developing atomic weapons
  (2) prevent Adolf Hitler from returning to power in Germany
  (3) stop the spread of communism in Western Europe
  (4) force Soviet satellite countries to break away from Soviet control

Base your answers to questions 38 and 39 on the quotation below and on your knowledge of social studies.

… We dare not forget today that we are the heirs of that first revolution. Let the word go forth from this time and place, to friend and foe alike, that the torch has been passed to a new generation of Americans— born in this century, tempered by war, disciplined by a hard and bitter peace, proud of our ancient heritage—and unwilling to witness or permit the slow undoing of those human rights to which this nation has always been committed, and to which we are committed today at home and around the world.…

To those people in the huts and villages of half the globe struggling to break the bonds of mass misery, we pledge our best efforts to help them help themselves, for whatever period is required—not because the communists may be doing it, not because we seek their votes, but because it is right. If a free society cannot help the many who are poor, it cannot save the few who are rich.…

— President John F. Kennedy, Inaugural Address, January 20, 1961

38 According to this quotation, President Kennedy wanted to
  (1) assert United States leadership in world affairs
  (2) follow a policy of neutrality
  (3) adopt appeasement as a foreign policy
  (4) abandon the policy of containment

39 Which foreign policy action by President Kennedy was intended to relieve the human suffering described in this quotation?
  (1) creating the Peace Corps
  (2) authorizing a naval blockade of Cuba
  (3) meeting with Soviet Premier Nikita Khrushchev in Vienna
  (4) negotiating the Nuclear Test Ban Treaty

40 A major goal of President Lyndon B. Johnson's Great Society program was to
(1) expand foreign aid
(2) eliminate poverty
(3) win the Vietnam War
(4) promote space exploration

Base your answer to question 41 on the newspaper headlines below and on your knowledge of social studies.

NIXON RESIGNS

HE URGES A TIME OF 'HEALING';
FORD WILL TAKE OFFICE TODAY

Source: New York Times, August 9, 1974

41 Which constitutional provision is most clearly illustrated by these headlines?
(1) presidential power
(2) qualifications to be president
(3) presidential succession
(4) advice and consent of the Senate

42 "… There is one sign the Soviets can make that would be unmistakable, that would advance dramatically the cause of freedom and peace. General Secretary Gorbachev, if you seek peace, if you seek prosperity for the Soviet Union and Eastern Europe, if you seek liberalization: Come here to this gate! Mr. Gorbachev, open this gate! Mr. Gorbachev, tear down this wall!…"
— President Ronald Reagan, June 12, 1987

President Reagan was calling for the end of the
(1) nuclear arms race
(2) Soviet invasion of Afghanistan
(3) division of Berlin, Germany
(4) Warsaw Pact

43 What was the central issue in both the John Peter Zenger case (1734–1735) and the controversy over the Pentagon Papers (1971)?
(1) right to bear arms
(2) freedom of religion
(3) freedom of the press
(4) right to counsel

Base your answer to question 44 on the poster below and on your knowledge of social studies.

Source: Library of Congress, 1978

44 What was one result of the boycott called for on the poster?
(1) The sale of lettuce and grapes increased.
(2) The power of large landowners over their laborers grew.
(3) Federal troops were sent to suppress violence on farms in the West.
(4) Public support for the goals of farmworkers increased.

45 "Convention Meets at Seneca Falls"
"19th Amendment Ratified"
"Betty Friedan Organizes National Organization for Women"

Which statement about women in the United States is best illustrated by these headlines?
(1) The role of women in society has remained unchanged since colonial times.
(2) The struggle for women's rights has spanned many decades.
(3) The earnings of women today are equal to those of men.
(4) The movement for women's rights has lacked leadership.

Base your answers to questions 46 and 47 on the graphs below and on your knowledge of social studies.

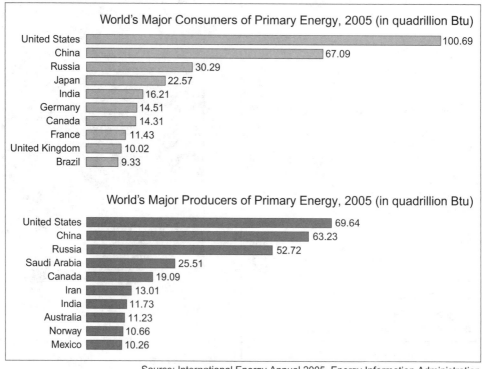

Source: International Energy Annual 2005, Energy Information Administration,
Department of Energy (adapted)

46 Which conclusion is best supported by the information on these graphs?
   (1) More nations produce energy than consume it.
   (2) South American nations are the greatest producers of energy.
   (3) Nations that produce the most energy are the richest nations in the world.
   (4) The United States uses more energy than it produces.

47 One result of the situation shown on the graphs is that the United States
   (1) must consider its need for energy when making foreign policy decisions
   (2) relies mainly on European nations for its energy
   (3) leads the world in the production of oil and steel
   (4) must find markets for its surplus energy

Base your answer to question 48 on the cartoon below and on your knowledge of social studies.

Source: Jim Morin, Miami Herald, in New York Times, September 10, 1989

48 Which statement most accurately expresses the main idea of the cartoon?
   (1) Successive presidents have failed to deal effectively with illegal drug use.
   (2) These presidents were successful in fighting the war on drugs.
   (3) The war on drugs was the major domestic concern of these presidents.
   (4) Many presidents have proposed legislation to decriminalize illegal drugs.

49 One way in which the Hayes-Tilden election of 1876 and the Bush-Gore election of 2000 are similar is that in each election the winner was
   (1) selected by the state legislatures
   (2) elected without a majority of the popular vote
   (3) aided by a third-party candidate
   (4) chosen by the United States Supreme Court

50 • Theodore Roosevelt mediates adoption of the Treaty of Portsmouth.
   • Richard Nixon visits China.
   • Bill Clinton supports peace accords in Northern Ireland.

These actions are examples of various presidents acting as
   (1) chief diplomat
   (2) head of party
   (3) chief legislator
   (4) commander in chief

PART II: THEMATIC ESSAY QUESTION

Directions: Write a well-organized essay that includes an introduction, several paragraphs addressing the task below, and a conclusion.

Theme: Government (Congressional Legislation)

> Throughout United States history, Congress has passed legislation to address important political, social, or economic issues. These laws have often had a significant impact on American society.

Task:

> Select *two* laws passed by the United States Congress and for *each*
> • Discuss the historical circumstances that led to the passage of the law
> • Discuss the impacts of the law on American society

You may use any federal law that was intended to address an important issue from your study of United States history. Some suggestions you might wish to consider include:

Embargo Act (1807)	Pure Food and Drug Act (1906)
Indian Removal Act (1830)	Social Security Act (1935)
Kansas-Nebraska Act (1854)	GI Bill/Servicemen's Readjustment Act (1944)
Interstate Commerce Act (1887)	Americans with Disabilities Act (1990)

You are *not* limited to these suggestions.
You may *not* discuss constitutional amendments.

Guidelines:

In your essay, be sure to:
  • Develop all aspects of the task
  • Support the theme with relevant facts, examples, and details
  • Use a logical and clear plan of organization, including an introduction and a conclusion that are beyond a restatement of the theme

 In developing your answer to Part II, be sure to keep this general definition in mind:

 (a) <u>discuss</u> means "to make observations about something using facts, reasoning, and argument; to present in some detail"

In developing your answers to Part III, be sure to keep these general definitions in mind:
  (a) <u>describe</u> means "to illustrate something in words or tell about it"
  (b) <u>discuss</u> means "to make observations about something using facts, reasoning, and argument; to present in some detail"

PART III: DOCUMENT-BASED QUESTION

This question is based on the accompanying documents. The question is designed to test your ability to work with historical documents. Some of these documents have been edited for the purposes of this question. As you analyze the documents, take into account the source of each document and any point of view that may be presented in the document.

Historical Context:

After World War II, the American people looked forward to a period of peace and prosperity. However, key events of the 1950s challenged that national mood and had significant social, economic, and political effects on the United States in the 1960s and beyond. These events included the **Korean War**, the **Montgomery bus boycott**, and the **launching of *Sputnik***.

Task:

Using the information from the documents and your knowledge of United States history, answer the questions that follow each document in Part A. Your answers to the questions will help you write the Part B essay in which you will be asked to

Choose *two* events of the 1950s identified in the historical context and for *each*
• Describe the historical circumstances surrounding the event
• Discuss the effects of the event on the United States and/or on American society

PART A — SHORT-ANSWER QUESTIONS

Directions: Analyze the documents and answer the short-answer questions that follow each document in the space provided.

Document 1

In [South] Korea the Government forces, which were armed to prevent border raids and to preserve internal security, were attacked by invading forces from North Korea. The Security Council of the United Nations called upon the invading troops to cease hostilities and to withdraw to the 38th parallel. This they have not done, but on the contrary have pressed the attack. The Security Council called upon all members of the United Nations to render every assistance to the United Nations in the execution of this resolution. In these circumstances I have ordered United States air and sea forces to give the Korean Government troops cover and support....

Source: President Harry Truman, Statement on the Situation in Korea, June 27, 1950

1 According to President Harry Truman, what was *one* reason he ordered United States forces to support South Korean government troops in 1950? [1]

_____

_____

Score ☐

Document 2a

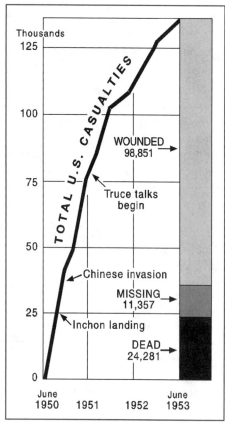

Source: "Korea: Three Years of War," Time,
June 29, 1953 (adapted)

Document 2b

... Within a year of the start of the international conflict in Korea, the number of people serving in America's armed forces more than doubled to over 3.2 million; army divisions went from ten to eighteen; the Air Force went from fortytwo to seventy-two wing groups; and the Navy expanded its number of ships from 600 to over 1,000. The pace of military build-up at this point exceeded that set by America when it first entered the Second World War. The bureaucracy of the Central Intelligence Agency (CIA) also mushroomed. In 1949 the CIA's Office of Policy Coordination had 302 personnel in its offices. By 1952 it had about 6,000. CIA stations in foreign countries increased from seven in 1951 to forty-seven in early 1953....

Source: Steven Hugh Lee, The Korean War,
Pearson Education Limited, 2001 (adapted)

2 Based on these documents, what were **two** effects of the Korean War on the United States? [2]

(1) _____

_____

Score ☐

(2) _____

_____

Score ☐

Document 3

> ... Complaints from African-American soldiers about Army racism led the NAACP [National Association for the Advancement of Colored People] to send civil rights activist and lawyer Thurgood Marshall to Korea in early 1951 to investigate. Marshall discovered that the Twenty-Fourth Infantry Regiment was the target of a disproportional amount of courts martial, and that the punishments meted [handed] out were much harsher than those given to non-African Americans. In his report, entitled 'Summary Justice: The Negro GI in Korea', Marshall underlined the fact that institutionalized segregation was responsible for much of the unfair treatment of black troops in Korea....
>
> The Korean War thus provided the crisis that finally pushed a reluctant Army to begin implementing policy recommendations made in [President Harry Truman's] Executive Order 9981. Policies which had been articulated [stated] earlier in the Cold War were now put into practice. Desegregation in the forces did not end discrimination, but it represented an important step towards greater equality for African Americans. The experiences of African-American soldiers in Korea thus benefitted from, and contributed to, the broader domestic movement for greater racial equality....

Source: Steven Hugh Lee, *The Korean War,* Pearson Education Limited, 2001

3a According to Steven Hugh Lee, what did Thurgood Marshall discover about the treatment of African American soldiers in Korea? [1]

_____

Score ☐

3b According to Steven Hugh Lee, what was *one* effect of the Korean War on American society? [1]

_____

Score ☐

Document 4

Inez Jessie Baskin comments on her experience using the bus system in Montgomery, Alabama, before the bus boycott that started in December 1955.

> ... I took the bus to work every day. Our bus system was segregated just like practically everything else. There was no specific line of demarcation separating seats reserved for white and black passengers. It was usually at the bus driver's discretion, and it varied depending on time of day and the driver, but you were just supposed to know. One thing was for certain, when a white person occupied a seat, even if it was one man to an entire long seat, blacks had to walk right on past. About six o'clock one evening, I received a phone call from a friend's mother telling me to go to the Dexter Avenue Church. That's where I heard about Rosa Parks' arrest. I had first met Rosa Parks during the time that I was a member of the NAACP. She had always impressed me. She was just an angel walking. When things happened that would upset most people, she would just give you this angelic smile, and that was the end of that. When I arrived, a small group of people were gathered in the church basement, and they were already talking about boycotting the local bus system and spreading some leaflets around about it....

Source: Jennings and Brewster, *The Century,* Doubleday, 1998

4 According to Inez Jessie Baskin, why were African Americans unhappy with the Montgomery bus system? [1]

_____

Score ☐

Document 5a

During the bus boycott in Montgomery, Alabama, many African American residents carpooled to work.

Source: Clayborne Carson et al., *Civil Rights Chronicle: The African-American Struggle for Freedom,*
Publications International

Document 5b

… Officials of the Montgomery City Lines, a subsidiary of National City Lines of Chicago have declined to say publicly how the boycott has affected the company financially. But a 50 per cent increase in bus fares—from 10 to 15 cents—and curtailed operations have offset the loss of business to some extent.

Before the boycott began last Dec. 5, approximately 65 per cent of the bus lines' passengers were Negroes [African Americans]. Since then, an estimated 75 per cent or more of the Negro customers have stopped riding.

Car pools operating with military precision have been organized to get Negroes to and from work. Negro taxicabs have done a thriving business. Police Commissioner Clyde Sellers says many Negroes have complained they are threatened with harm if they rode the buses.… Negro leaders led by a 27-year-old Baptist minister, the Rev. Martin Luther King Jr., demanded a "first come, first serve" arrangement which would seat Negroes from the rear and white passengers from the front until all seats were taken.

Under the present arrangement, the dividing line is determined by the driver. Bus company officials rejected the "first come" proposal.…

Source: *Montgomery Advertiser*, February 19, 1956 (adapted)

5 Based on these documents, what were *two* effects of the Montgomery bus boycott on Montgomery, Alabama? [2]

(1) _____

_____

Score ☐

(2) _____

_____

Score ☐

Document 6a

... The idea so long cherished by Southern whites — and by many Northerners too — that the Southern Negro (whether through ignorance or intimidation or a shrewd recognition of reality) was content with the way things were, that only a handful of agitators opposed the system of segregation, was swept aside by the mass marches, demonstrations, meetings. Montgomery had been the first sign of this, and now it was made clear beyond argument that Negroes all across the South had only been waiting for an opportunity to end their long silence....

The sit-ins were an important learning experience for white Southerners, and also for those Northerners who were convinced of some mystical, irremovable germ of prejudice in the Southern mind: when the first lunch-counters were desegregated, the world did not come to an end. Whites and Negroes could use public facilities together, it was shown, without violent repercussions, without white withdrawal. Southern whites, once a new pattern became accepted and established in the community, would conform to it as they conformed to the old. Men and women seeking a sandwich at a lunch counter, as young Negroes could see readily in many of the sit-ins, were more interested in satisfying their hunger or their thirst than in who sat next to them. After two months of desegregation in Winston Salem, North Carolina, the manager of a large store said: "You would think it had been going on for fifty years. I am tickled to death over the situation."...

Source: Howard Zinn, *SNCC: The New Abolitionists,* Beacon Press

Document 6b

Source: Greensboro Record, February 2, 1960

6 Based on these documents, what was *one* effect of the Montgomery bus boycott on American society? [1]

_____

_____

Score ☐

Document 7

Nikita Sergeyevich Khrushchev [Soviet leader] was almost desperate to beat the Americanskis at something. *Anything.* He boasted that communism would bury capitalism, later claiming he meant only by becoming richer and more productive, not by engaging in war. But how long might that take? Fifty years? A hundred? He needed something now. And in the summer of 1955, at about the time he returned from the Geneva conference, where [President Dwight] Eisenhower had urged the Open Skies proposal on him, some of Khrushchev's scientific advisers informed him of an interesting development.

In the course of reading American science journals, they had learned that the United States had begun a project to put an artificial satellite into orbit in 1958, as part of its contribution to the International Geophysical Year. An orbiting satellite had obvious military possibilities, but the foolish Americans had decided not to make it a military project—they wanted it to be peaceful and scientific. We can beat them to it, the scientists told Khrushchev, because we're already developing the rocket.

The Soviet Union's hydrogen bomb was enormous, and in 1955 its engineers and technicians were working on the design of a huge liquid-fueled rocket powerful enough to carry it five thousand miles. With some modifications, said the scientists, we can use the rocket to put a small satellite into orbit long before it will be ready to carry an H-bomb. Khrushchev saw a possibility here that nobody in Washington had seen—the chance to score the propaganda coup of the century. The Soviet satellite, code-named *Sputnik* ("Fellow Traveler"), got his enthusiastic "*Da!*" [*Yes!*]…

Source: Geoffrey Perret, *Eisenhower,* Random House, 1999 (adapted)

7 According to Geoffrey Perret, what was **one** reason the Soviet Union was interested in putting a satellite into orbit? [1]

_____

_____

Score ☐

Document 8

On September 2, 1958, less than a year after the launching of *Sputnik*, President Dwight Eisenhower signed into law the National Defense Education Act (NDEA).

> ... Between 1958 and 1968, NDEA also provided loan money for more than 1.5 million individual college students—fellowships directly responsible for producing 15,000 Ph.D.s a year. NDEA allocated approximately $1 billion to support research and education in the sciences over four years; federal support for science-related research and education increased between 21 and 33 percent per year through 1964, representing a tripling of science research and education expenditures over five years. States were given money to strengthen schools on a fifty-fifty matching basis, thousands of teachers were sent to NDEA-sponsored summer schools, and the National Science Foundation sponsored no fewer than fifty-three curriculum development projects. By the time of the lunar landing in 1969, NDEA alone had pumped $3 billion into American education....

Source: Paul Dickson, *Sputnik: The Shock of the Century*, Walker Publishing Company, 2001

8 According to Paul Dickson, what were **two** effects of the launching of *Sputnik* on education in the United States? [2]

(1) _____

Score ☐

(2) _____

Score ☐

Document 9

> ... First, I believe that this nation should commit itself to achieving the goal, before this decade is out, of landing a man on the moon and returning him safely to the earth. No single space project in this period will be more impressive to mankind, or more important for the long-range exploration of space; and none will be so difficult or expensive to accomplish. We propose to accelerate the development of the appropriate lunar space craft. We propose to develop alternate liquid and solid fuel boosters, much larger than any now being developed, until certain which is superior. We propose additional funds for other engine development and for unmanned explorations — explorations which are particularly important for one purpose which this nation will never overlook: the survival of the man who first makes this daring flight. But in a very real sense, it will not be one man going to the moon — if we make this judgment affirmatively, it will be an entire nation. For all of us must work to put him there.... Third, an additional 50 million dollars will make the most of our present leadership, by accelerating the use of space satellites for world-wide communications. Fourth, an additional 75 million dollars — of which 53 million dollars is for the Weather Bureau — will help give us at the earliest possible time a satellite system for world-wide weather observation....

Source: President John F. Kennedy, Special Message to Congress, May 25, 1961

9 According to President John F. Kennedy, why was spending money on space projects important for the United States? [1]

_____

_____

Score ☐

PART B — ESSAY

Directions: Write a well-organized essay that includes an introduction, several paragraphs, and a conclusion. Use evidence from *at least four* documents in your essay. Support your response with relevant facts, examples, and details. Include additional outside information.

Historical Context:

> After World War II, the American people looked forward to a period of peace and prosperity. However, key events of the 1950s challenged that national mood and had significant social, economic, and political effects on the United States in the 1960s and beyond. These events included the **Korean War**, the **Montgomery bus boycott**, and the **launching of Sputnik**.

Task:

Using the information from the documents and your knowledge of United States history, write an essay in which you

> Choose *two* events of the 1950s identified in the historical context and for *each*
>
> • Describe the historical circumstances surrounding the event
> • Discuss the effects of the event on the United States and/or on American society

Guidelines:

In your essay, be sure to

• Develop all aspects of the task
• Incorporate information from *at least four* documents
• Incorporate relevant outside information
• Support the theme with relevant facts, examples, and details
• Use a logical and clear plan of organization, including an introduction and a conclusion that are beyond a restatement of the theme